THE PATH OF THE SOUL AFTER DEATH

IN CRISTO MORIMUR

PER SPIRITUM SANCTUM

EX DEO NASCIMUR

REVIVISCIMUS

THE PATH OF THE SOUL AFTER DEATH

The Community of the Living and the Dead as Witnessed by Rudolf Steiner in His Eulogies and Funeral Addresses

PETER SELG

2011
STEINERBOOKS

SteinerBooks
610 Main Street, Great Barrington, MA 01230
www.steinerbooks.org

Translated by Catherine E. Creeger.

Originally published in German by Verlag am Goetheanum as
*Rudolf Steiners Toten-Gedenken. Die Verstorbenen, der Dornacher
Bau und die Anthroposophische Gesellschaft.*

Library of Congress Cataloging-in-Publication Data

Selg, Peter, 1963-
 [Rudolf Steiners Toten-Gedenken. English]
 The path of the soul after death : the community of the living and the
dead as witnessed by Rudolf Steiner in his eulogies and funeral addresses
/ Peter Selg.
     p. cm.
 Includes bibliographical references.
 ISBN 978-0-88010-724-2
 1. Steiner, Rudolf, 1861-1925. 2. Future life—Anthroposophy.
3. Eulogies—History and criticism. 4. Funeral orations—History and
criticism. I. Title.
  BP596.F85S4613 2010
  236'.2--dc22
                                    2010032072

Printed in the United States

*When we approach the spiritual world with the conscious-
ness that spirit eyes look down on us and test our relationship to world truth, and we are aware of spirit ears
that hear the truth or falsehood in our hearts, we develop
a feeling of responsibility toward the perception of the
spiritual world that results. When this feeling develops
into concrete communion with those who once worked
alongside us and now continue to work with us in the
streaming of our souls, the spiritual-scientific worldview
and movement become the living bridge between worlds
that will never be connected in any other way, neither now
nor in all times to come.*[1]

— RUDOLF STEINER

Contents

Preface

At this point in the pursuit of anthroposophical spiritual science, our souls should be able to hear the insistent words of our precious dead: *"Perceive the spiritual world! Its gifts to humankind include the possibility of uniting the dead and the living."*[2]

RUDOLF STEINER SAW RELATIONSHIPS with the dead as "the religious attitude of the future" in "the highest sense of the word": "In ancient times, the religious sense in the human soul was aroused primarily through feeling. Now, however, we are approaching a time when our spirituality will have to be enlivened and kindled by the earth's connection to the spiritual world. We must become ever more concrete in our spiritual activity and receptive to seeking the spirit in concrete realities. We must recognize that after human individualities pass through the portal of death, they continue to work with forces developed here during earthly life. Becoming comfortable with thinking and speaking of the dead as concretely as we speak of the living will affect human activity profoundly. It will ennoble our attitudes toward each other, imbuing them with morality in the truest sense of the word and with divine substance that will then surge and flow through human life. We must keep all this in mind in the future if we are to truly take the mission and task of anthroposophical spiritual science into our hearts and souls."[3] According to Rudolf Steiner, the "enlivening" and even the "sanctification" of earthly existence are not only directly connected to our relationship to death and the deceased; in fact, that relationship deepens them and makes them altogether possible. In this respect, says Steiner, anthroposophical spiritual science has a specific cultural task or "mission," namely, to uphold the image of the individual beyond the threshold of death—in other words, to create a genuine anthropology that acknowledges the existence of individual beings even in the post-death state and acts out of this knowledge to shape connections to them. *"We are separated from the spiritual worlds only by states of consciousness, not by spatial circumstances. States of consciousness are what separate us."*[4]

Rudolf Steiner not only taught the new spiritual science of anthroposophy, he also lived it. His life story and life's work must be seen in connection to the spiritual world and thus also to the earthly "dead" whose metamorphosed existence Steiner was already able to perceive in his youth. In his *Autobiography*, Steiner looks back on his years as a student in Vienna and writes:

> At that time I felt obliged to seek the truth through philosophy. Although I was supposedly studying mathematics and science, I was convinced I would be unable to relate to them if their findings were not solidly grounded in philosophy. I, however, beheld a spiritual world *as a reality*. I could clearly see the spiritual individuality of each person, which united with the physical germ originating from the parents; that person's physical body and activity in the physical world were simply manifestations of the spiritual individuality. When someone died, I was able to trace that individual's progress into the spiritual world. Once, after the death of a classmate, I wrote about this aspect of my inner life to one of my former teachers who had maintained a friendship with me after my graduation from secondary school. His reply, although unusually cordial, contained no mention of what I had written about my deceased classmate."[5]

Later, even many of the theosophists and anthroposophists who acknowledged and revered Rudolf Steiner as their spiritual teacher were surprised by the "realness" of his relationship to the dead. Although this relationship far exceeded what they themselves could achieve or even comprehend, they experienced it as both exemplary and prophetic. As an example or model to follow, Steiner's life was both unusual and exceptional. Although civilization stood on the brink of catastrophe in the early twentieth century, Steiner characterized this time as the beginning of an "Age of Light," in line with the predictions of both ancient and modern esotericism. As Hölderlin wrote, "Many timid eyes are waiting to behold the light."[6] Shortly after Steiner's death on March 30, 1925, Friedrich Rittelmeyer wrote, "Of all the Christians we knew, Rudolf Steiner was the first to whom heaven was revealed on earth."[7]

*

Within the Anthroposophical Society, Rudolf Steiner not only spoke frequently about death and the continued existence of the human soul, he also founded a new type of community, a union of spiritually active human souls that endured beyond death. When eulogizing deceased anthroposophists, Rudolf Steiner spoke repeatedly of "perceiving our community."[8] The Anthroposophical Society was both a working instrument of anthroposophy and a spiritual union of individuals who received this new science of the spirit into the depths of their souls and carried it with them into the spiritual world after their earthly deaths. In one lecture Steiner said, "In our movement, the most significant factors linking individual souls to it are noted as a matter of course. Such observations allow us to learn what connects human souls to the world as a whole after death. Also, for us, observing the character of soul life after death is easiest with regard to souls related to our movement."[9] Immersing ourselves in the eulogics of deceased anthroposophists that

Rudolf Steiner gave in lecture halls or at the cemeteries, as well as in his other statements about the death of colleagues and their after-death existence, yields profound impressions of his meaning and intentions, of the spiritual nature of both the individual and the community, and thus also of the essence of the Anthroposophical Society that Steiner understood as *"our community."* Ultimately, too, this perspective also sheds new light on the "building for the anthroposophical cause," the Goetheanum, in Dornach, since so many deceased members had been involved in its development.

My purpose here is to deepen awareness of these connections. How Rudolf Steiner commemorated the dead, his choice of words, and the inner processes that he described—sometimes in great detail—make clear the extent to which his addresses were shaped by his connections to the deceased and related to their new stage of existence. In this sense, any genuine memorial address not only recapitulates a biography, but also assists the deceased on the path after death. And it serves this latter function in harmony with the ritual performed by the priest, which, Rudolf Steiner emphasized, is indispensable.

Inasmuch as Rudolf Steiner's words were attuned to human soul development after death, their true depth and meaning can be understood only against the background of an anthropological study of the period immediately after death. For this reason, the second part of the book covers the central aspects of anthroposophical research into human life after death.

PETER SELG

Director of the Ita Wegman Institute
for Basic Research into Anthroposophy

I

"Our Community"

I: Rudolf Steiner (1861–1925)

1

Rudolf Steiner's Eulogies

We will grasp anthroposophy's task when we understand that we must eliminate the abyss separating us from the dead.[10]

ALREADY QUITE EARLY IN HIS LIFE—when he was still a student—Rudolf Steiner was asked to give a eulogy (for Joseph Eduard Fehr of Vienna, whom he had never actually met in person, yet, in an unusual way, he knew well[11]). Later, also, Steiner was frequently asked to speak at interments at the request of friends and family members of the deceased, regardless of their religious affiliations—for example, at the burial of his close associate Ludwig Jacobowski, a Jewish man of letters, in 1900 in Berlin. By 1912 at the latest, Rudolf Steiner was giving addresses at memorial services for theosophical and anthroposophical friends. In the majority of these cases, Rudolf Steiner was asked to supplement the words of the priest or pastor in the context of a traditional denominational (Protestant or Catholic) funeral service.

Christian Morgenstern's cremation service on April 4, 1914 in Basel was organized entirely by Steiner, in accordance with Morgenstern's wishes. Rudolf Steiner gave the main address, which was both inspiring and moving.[12] This farewell ceremony was unusual because Morgenstern had explicitly requested no church funeral and no pastor but rather an event organized by Rudolf Steiner, his spiritual teacher and friend.[13]

In the late fall and winter of 1918/1919, Rudolf Steiner presented the anthroposophist and Catholic priest Hugo Schuster with the text of a new interment ritual.[14] It was then performed for the first time in Arlesheim on January 14, 1919, at the funeral of Marie Leyh, followed by a funeral address given by Steiner.[15] Years later, Rudolf Steiner stressed that this ritual had been developed "in the sense of our Christian Community."[16] Moreover, he emphasized to the founders of The Christian Community that *"this ritual is the best means of guiding the soul of the deceased from the world of physical existence into the world of spiritual existence.*"[17] On June 27, 1924, in Dornach, Rudolf Steiner spoke about the reality of the funeral service as conducted by an ordained priest:[18]

> You watch the service unfold. You see the coffin contain-ing the earthly remains of the deceased and the specific ritual performed in front of it. You hear the priest speaking prayer-like formulas. The ritual could be more complex, but its present simplicity adequately captures what it is meant to achieve for humanity. And what is that?
>
> My dear friends, suppose there is a mirror here and some object or being over there. In addition to the thing itself, you see its reflection in the mirror. These two elements are also present during a funeral service. The ritual conducted by the priest in front of the coffin is only a reflection. It is truly a reflection; it would not be a reality if it were not a reflection. And what does it reflect? The ritual the priest performs here in front of the body is an image of the original in the adjacent suprasensible world. While we are performing the ritual of earthly farewell here, in front of the physical body and the etheric body (which is actually still present), the beings on the other side of existence are performing a heavenly rite of reception for the soul and spirit. Our ritual possesses truth only if it originates in that reality. Any genuine funeral ritual we perform corresponds to a suprasensible rite, and the two work together. If the funeral prayer is filled with reverence, truth, and dignity, it resonates with the prayers of the beings of higher hier-archies in the suprasensible world, and the spiritual world and the physical world come together.[19]

After The Christian Community was founded and began its work in the fall of 1922, Rudolf Steiner did not hesitate to refer any anthroposophists who sought advice about organiz-ing a funeral service but were not themselves affiliated with any particular denomination to this "movement for religious renewal." He declined to organize services himself in favor of the newly formulated funeral ritual he had presented to The Christian Community.[20] Either as part of or following Christian Community funeral services, however, Steiner continued to give eulogies for the dead when asked, as he did at the funeral of the painter Hermann Linde on June 29, 1923. Friedrich Doldinger, a young Christian Community priest, conducted the funeral service to Rudolf Steiner's great satisfaction: *"A strong stream of inner, truly effective devotion flowed from how we were able to accompany Hermann Linde to cremation."*[21] Two weeks after Linde's funeral, Rudolf Steiner spoke to the priests of The Christian Community about further collaboration:

> On such social occasions sanctified by religious ritual, I will never again undertake anything without the participation of this religious movement [that is, of The Christian Community]. I will no longer speak at funerals alone, without a priest. *The ritual must be performed.*[22]

Friedrich Doldinger also performed the last funeral service at which Rudolf Steiner was able to be present and give an address—Edith Maryon's funeral on May 6, 1924, in Basel. Two days earlier, Rudolf Steiner had telegraphed his request to Doldinger:

> Can you come Tuesday 11 o'clock Maryon cremation?
> Rudolf Steiner.

Knowing of Rudolf Steiner's close and even esoteric connection with Maryon, who had been named to the Executive Council of the Anthroposophical Society and entrusted with the Section for Fine Arts, Doldinger asked Rudolf Steiner's advice on how to proceed in this particular instance. He received this reply: *"You conduct the service for the deceased as a member of*

*the human race. The ritual must come first, and after that I will
talk about specific circumstances, which—as you know—were
anthroposophical in this case.*"[23]

Rudolf Steiner informed the class members of Edith Maryon's
death at the beginning of the esoteric lesson of the Free School of
Spiritual Science on May 2. Already in earlier years, either soon
after hearing of a member's death or during a general assem-
bly, Steiner had spoken to members of the Anthroposophical
Society about deceased colleagues in ways both personal and
beyond personal. Edith Maryon's death and Doldinger's inquiry,
however, fell into the time of transition right after the Christmas
Conference and occurred within a specific spiritual connection.
Never before and never again did Rudolf Steiner speak about a
deceased anthroposophist in this way, during an esoteric lesson
and in the context of spiritual community-building.

*

Not only in eulogies for individuals but also in his anthroposophical lectures on death and relationships to the dead, Rudolf
Steiner pointed out repeatedly that a forward-looking approach
to the phenomenon of death would not entail any "desanctifica-
tion" of the "mystery of death" but simply an acknowledging of
it as a "metamorphosis in the mode of life," a change in how the
departed individuality lived life. In this context, Steiner spoke of
the need for a *"metamorphosis of love"*:

> This is truly practical anthroposophy for the soul. When
> we know, and know in the right way, that death is not the
> destroyer of life but rather the beginning of a new mode
> of life, we must also be able to explain that when someone
> "dies" as far as earthly life is concerned, the love bestowed
> on that individual also enters a new mode of existence. If we
> do not understand this metamorphosis of love, we cannot
> really claim to understand death as a metamorphosis of

life as we profess to understand it within a spiritual movement such as the anthroposophical movement.[24]

At the present stage of humanity's development, said Rudolf Steiner, it is important to develop a different connection to death and to the dead during earthly life: *"We must learn not only to think differently about death but also to feel differently about it."*[25]

This is all the more important because the dead have a concrete need for those still alive on earth. Connections established on earth, said Steiner, remain in effect and are indispensably important to the existence and future of the deceased. The memories and spiritual thoughts of friends still alive on earth are the substance that nourishes human souls who have passed into the spiritual world. At night, the thoughts of the living are sought out by the dead who are connected to them. In one lecture, Rudolf Steiner put it like this:

> When clairvoyant vision sees dead souls, sleeping human souls are revealed as fertile ground for the dead, for our departed. To anyone looking into the spiritual world for the first time, it is not merely surprising but actually shattering to see how human souls in life between death and rebirth rush toward sleeping souls in search of the thoughts and ideas those sleeping souls contain. The dead are nourished by these thoughts; they need this food. When we fall asleep in the evening, we can tell ourselves that the ideas and thoughts that pass through our consciousness when we are awake now begin to come alive. They become living beings, so to speak. Dead souls come to take part in these ideas and feel nourished by perceiving them.
>
> When we turn our clairvoyant vision toward deceased human beings as they return each night to the sleeping friends they left behind (and in fact, they do return not only to blood relatives but also to friends) and attempt to nourish themselves on the thoughts and ideas these friends

carry with them into sleep, we see how shattering it is to
the dead when they find nothing there to nourish them.
Our ideas vary greatly, and not all of them are equally
suited to nourishing the dead as we sleep.[26]

Rudolf Steiner spoke of "soul starvation" afflicting the dead
in the spiritual world as a result of our materialistic feeling and
perceiving. From the perspective of the history of consciousness,
he continues:

We find that interaction between the living and the dead
is becoming increasingly difficult. Only a relatively short
time ago, this interaction was much easier. When the
Christians of the Middle Ages, or even of centuries not
long past, turned in prayer toward their deceased relatives or acquaintances, their feelings were much stronger
in terms of being able to make their way up to the souls of
the dead than is now the case, at least among those who
succumb to contemporary external trends. In the past, it
was much easier for deceased souls to feel imbued with the
warm breath of love from those who looked up to them in
prayer or in thought. Today the dead are much more cut
off from the living than they were only a relatively short
time ago, and it is much more difficult for them to glimpse
what is alive in the souls of those left behind. This difficulty
is a fact of humanity's evolution. Finding our way back
to this vital interaction between the living and the dead,
however, must also become a fact of evolution. In earlier
times, it was still natural for human souls to experience
a vital connection to the dead, although that connection
was no longer fully conscious because the clairvoyance
that formerly made it possible to trace the life of the dead
had long since been lost. Today, the interaction with the
dead that once came naturally can be regained by internalizing thoughts and ideas about the higher, spiritual worlds.

This effort leads to the strength needed to reestablish living connections to the dead. Thus one of the practical tasks of anthroposophical activity is to rebuild the bridge from the living to the dead through spiritual science.[27]

According to Rudolf Steiner, it is urgently important *"for western spiritual development to gradually overcome death—on the cognitive level—by recognizing it as a transformation of life itself."*[28]

*

As he expressed repeatedly and emphatically, Rudolf Steiner saw gradual, ongoing construction of the "bridge" between the living and the dead (in contemporary form and under modern premises) as one of the central tasks of anthroposophy and as a "factor in humanity's spiritual culture."[29] According to Steiner, the task of anthroposophical spiritual science is to spiritualize human feeling as well as human thinking, and in that process to develop the soul "substance" the dead need as a prerequisite to their "vital interaction," their ongoing supportive activity in the earthly realm. "We will grasp the task of anthroposophy when we understand that we must eliminate the abyss separating us from the dead."[30]

"When people die, it does not mean they leave us behind; we can remain in contact with them and be active on their behalf."[31] Rudolf Steiner describes overcoming the ever-widening "abyss" or "barrier" that separates the living from the dead as one of the central concerns of anthroposophical spiritual science. "It is essential to truly bridge the abyss that separates the living from the so-called dead, to increasingly unite those human beings incarnated in bodies with those who have assumed the modes of existence we experience between death and rebirth."[32] Modern spiritual science, said Steiner, must and will overcome the "gap" separating us from the world of the dead, not only in our consciousness but also in our soul life as a whole. Through anthroposophy and through the individuals uniting with and in it, a new bond will develop: "More and more, the barriers between the living and the dead will be broken down by this movement that brings willing individuals together under the sign of spiritual science."[33] For Rudolf Steiner, creating this bond was part of the actual purpose of the spiritual-scientific movement and a concrete indication of anthroposophy's "value for life."[34]

In elaborating on this subject, Rudolf Steiner left no doubt that he understood the anthroposophical community as a group of individuals charged with developing new and different ways of thinking, feeling, and willing with regard to the existence of the dead in the spiritual world. He obviously assumed that individuals united in anthroposophy would take up this clearly stated task that was to be accomplished in individual consciousness: "At this point in time, it is important to be clear that spiritual science is charged with developing this awareness that we belong together with souls who have died."[35] Rudolf Steiner's comments in this context were never elitist or exclusive in character. The point was to develop a new attitude and practical approach to the dead "so we can be of value to the dead through anthroposophy."[36] This new approach was to serve humanity as active preparation for a future stage of civilization. In many lectures and personal conversations, Rudolf Steiner offered both general and individual suggestions on how to relate to the dead—suggestions that took the form of exercises, verses, and other ways to approach and accompany the dead in soul and spirit. "In the time immediately after death, much of what a soul experiences and feels depends on the spiritual understanding of those who were close and remain behind on the physical plane."[37] Rudolf Steiner's suggestions fell on fertile ground; as he repeatedly appreciated, what he called "developing wholly different circumstances" around relating to the dead became a major force in the anthroposophical movement, both for individuals and in common activity.

Meine Liebe folge deiner Seele
Sie wärme dein Kaltsein
Sie mildere deine Hitze
Meine Seele bilde Gedanken
In denen deine Gedanken sind
Meine Seele hege Gefühle
In denen dein Geist webet.

2: Meditation by Rudolf Steiner for Dr. Hilma Walter
after the death of his mother (1924)

*

Rudolf Steiner described the need to be attentive to active forces from the spirit world of the dead not only in his actual eulogies and meditations for the dead but also in a variety of other contexts:

> Through these subtle, delicate manifestations that always arise between the spiritual world and our souls, we gradually learn to hear the voices of the dead, especially of those with specific karmic connections to us. We perceive them by directing our thoughts to them in the right way. In the inner atmosphere and aura of our souls where these thoughts gradually become perceptible, although perhaps in very quiet and intimate ways, we sense that those who have passed through the gate of death live on in us. They live with us, they take part in our destiny, and at the same time they lend their strength to everything that is best in us, to what we can become in the context of the world's functioning.[38]

It is the job of the living, according to Steiner, to accompany and support their dead friends and relatives, to provide the care and assistance the dead need. The connection between the "living" and the "dead," however, is reciprocal and mutually beneficial: *"At the same time they lend their strength to everything that is best in us, to what we can become in the context of the world's functioning."* Rudolf Steiner often spoke in concrete terms about living and working together with individuals who had crossed the threshold of death:

> The actions of the dead are interwoven with the feelings and will impulses of the so-called living. And that is actually history.
> Individuals do not stop being active in the human community when they pass through the portal of death.

They continue to be active, although not in the way they were active here in physical bodies. Although we live in the illusion that what we do flows from our own feelings and will impulses, many of our actions actually flow from the deeds of those who have crossed over.

Knowing that everything we do in the context of human community also happens in community with the dead will become a significant factor in human development in the future. Such awareness is based primarily on our life of feeling and willing, so of course it will also have to be grasped through feeling and will. Dry, abstract ideas will never allow us to grasp it, but ideas derived from the full scope of spiritual science will. Admittedly, people will have to get used to developing very different concepts about these things.[39]

Souls dead to the earthly realm work on in the feeling and willing of the living, with whom they form a certain unity: "We can feel nothing unless the dead are present in the realm of our feeling; we can will nothing unless the dead are likewise present in that realm."[40] *And that is actually history.*

*

Rudolf Steiner handled these connections with utmost clarity of consciousness. At various points in his lectures, he revealed the extent to which deceased individuals accompanied his life's work and even the unfolding of anthroposophy. He had been intimately involved in the aspirations and efforts of these individuals and was now taking them further: "In our spiritual efforts, we can rely on the dead much more than on the living."[41] In one lecture, Rudolf Steiner described his connection to Goethe's being and spiritual work, which he himself was continuing and from which he drew inspiration.[42] There Steiner said, "Tremendously much would be gained if that selflessness were to extend its reach somewhat further, so that those living later would connect to the dead and attempt to maintain continuity in evolution in a truly conscious way. Whether through pure relationships of choice or through other relationships brought about by karma, it is tremendously meaningful to consciously follow in the footsteps of those who are now attempting to allow their activity to radiate from the spiritual world."[43]

In future, according to Steiner, human attempts at collaboration will be enhanced, transcending the threshold of death in a common realm of destiny. Since the Mystery of Golgotha, this realm has been associated with the active Christ-being. "In the future, we will know that we are in contact with the dead in this realm of destiny, and we will know that this realm we share with the dead is also the realm of Christ. We will know that through the Mystery of Golgotha, Christ descended to become active on earth and to share with us what we share with the dead. This knowledge will become the norm, not the exception."[44] This shared, Christ-pervaded "realm" of the living and the dead, says Steiner, points to a common *language* that connects souls. He repeatedly described anthroposophical spiritual science as the language of the Christ under modern circumstances, as the word understood by the dead as well as the living, the word that unites and allows them to work together in dialogue.

*

Whether in branch meetings or in other forms of spiritual collaboration, Rudolf Steiner saw the anthroposophical community and its spiritual work in the light of this intention: "Today we feel not only that we are working on behalf of so-called living human beings but also that our spiritual-scientific work and the spread of anthroposophical activity serves the spiritual worlds."[45] In Bergen, Norway, on October 10, 1913, Steiner explained in greater detail:

1.) Die Auffassung des Todes: Die Menschenwesenheit entschwindet dem
gewöhnlichen Bewusstsein — sie wirkt nicht auf
die Sinne und nicht auf den Verstand = sie wird
Erinnerung und damit tritt sie ein in dasjenige,
was die überlebenden sind — der Tote verbindet

2.) Das Erfühlen des Todes: sich mit den überlebenden; diese begegnen
ihm auf der andern Seite des Lebens — sie
sind die Impulse für sein Rückwärts leben
nach dem geiste hin = an die Gestorbenen
schliessen sich als an einen Zug die Ueber-
lebenden im schlafenden Zustande an =

Was bedeutet die Wachhaltung der Erinnerung?
Dass der Tote wirksam sein kann =

3: Undated notebook entry by Rudolf Steiner

When we address living individuals during their waking life, we also satisfy their soul needs in the nocturnal state, and in that process we engender ideas that are fruitful food for souls destined to die before us. That is why we feel compelled to disseminate spiritual science or anthroposophy not only in the usual public ways but also in private, in our branches, because there is special value in doing so in person, in the physical company of individuals actively pursuing spiritual science. I have said that the dead can draw nourishment from the still incarnated souls of their companions during life. We are attempting to bring souls together to constantly expand the fertile ground available to the dead. For individuals who die after having been introduced to spiritual science, it is not uncommon to find this fertile ground not among their family members, who are all materialists, but in the souls of anthroposophists. This is the deeper reason for our work within the Society: We want to ensure that before members die, they meet others who will continue to be involved with spiritual matters on earth. In sleep, such people provide a source of nourishment for the dead.[46]

According to Rudolf Steiner, the anthroposophical community was working very concretely in this way to develop future social forms that would include both the living and the dead. These efforts were shaping the beginnings of new forms of spiritual affiliation and collaboration that transcend the bonds customarily uniting individuals with family and friends. In a world that had lost its ancient spiritual organization and now needed to develop new connections, including ones that would bridge the threshold of death, these new beginnings were available to everyone.

Thus the anthroposophical community was and is of greatest importance, said Steiner, and those working together in it remain connected even after they make the transition to the realm of the dead. From there, they continue to actively support the community. In Zurich in January of 1915, Rudolf Steiner said:

> When individuals pass through the portal of death into the spiritual world prematurely, it often seems to us as if they have done so with heartfelt love for our spiritual movement, in order to be able to help us by applying the stronger forces available to them in the spiritual world. The souls of many of our departed are filled with wonderfully clear perceptions of how essential our spiritual movement is. For those able to see into the spiritual world, all who have passed through the portal of death and now look down on the movement with which they were associated are like our movement's spiritual heralds, spiritual standard-bearers who call out to us unceasingly, "While we were united with you, we were convinced of the necessity of this movement. And now that we have entered the spiritual world, we know that we can and must provide help when this movement needs it.[47]

Rudolf Steiner counted himself as belonging to this anthroposophical movement and society, speaking repeatedly of *"our cause"* and *"our community."*

※

It often fell to Rudolf Steiner to convey news of a member's death to the anthroposophical community. Though he himself may have been surprised by a sudden crossing of the threshold, he accompanied it consciously, even from a great geographical distance. One day after Sophie Stinde's death on November 17, 1915 in Munich, Rudolf Steiner reported it to the members in Berlin, himself deeply affected by the event. At the beginning of his regular evening lecture, he said, "It is too soon to say much about this exceptionally difficult and significant loss to our Society, so I will say only a very few words about this event, which is so painful and momentous for us."[48] Very probably, Rudolf Steiner was surprised by Sophie Stinde's death. Like other weighty strokes of destiny—such as the burning of the Goetheanum—that befell him in the course of his life's work, its timing could not be ascertained through spiritual research. *"It is not for you to know the times or the seasons, which the Father hath put in his own power."* (Acts 1:7)

When he brought news of a death to the members of the Anthroposophical Society and anthroposophical community, Rudolf Steiner often included a brief biographical review of the person's life. Like his actual funeral addresses, these words were imbued with wisdom, modesty, and even a modern piety. Steiner stressed that the spiritual world stood behind the timing of an individual's death, which therefore had to be accepted: "As human beings, we are not allowed to think beyond what we are allotted as human beings, so to speak; we must realize that the prevailing wisdom of the world is wiser than we are."[49] In conveying news of deaths to members and in his memorial addresses, Rudolf Steiner created an image of the being of the departed, and he completely accompanied the deceased soul. He transcended the domain of personal sorrow without either abolishing or suppressing it.

At Christian Morgenstern's cremation, "his tears flowed freely," according to Marie von Sivers and Margareta Morgenstern. In his exceptionally brief acknowledgement of the death of Marie von Sivers' sister Olga, who died in Russia in 1917 while serving as a nurse in a military hospital, Rudolf Steiner said to members of the Anthroposophical Society, *"So far I have said little about one of the hardest losses of all, because I am too deeply involved and have lost too much myself. My personal connection to this loss does not allow me to touch on many of its aspects."*[50]

*

In his memorial addresses for deceased members of the Anthroposophical Society, Rudolf Steiner dwelt on the being of the one who had just passed into the spiritual world, creating an image focused on the individual's connection to anthroposophy as the central spiritual experience and relationship of a lifetime.

In these addresses, Steiner never drew conclusions about the destiny of the deceased; with very few exceptions, he did not mention, or even hint at, karmic connections. Although his knowledge of such connections was extensive, it had no place in his eulogies, which clearly focused on the deceased's path to anthroposophy and contributions to the anthroposophical movement.

"I was also privileged to see into this heart," was the extent of his comments on the tragic tone of Helene von Schewitz's life and his own insight into her destiny.[51] More was not forthcoming, at least not in his memorial address.

Rudolf Steiner spoke about many deceased members of the Anthroposophical Society, not only prominent personalities but also people whose life and work would never grace the pages of history books. In his addresses, it was obvious how attentively Rudolf Steiner perceived and accompanied each individual on his or her path to the anthroposophical community. *"Yes, we found you. Many years ago, you came and united with us."*[52] He often mentioned the first time he met the deceased, perhaps at an anthroposophical lecture or in conversation afterward, seeming to recall the encounter in great detail.

Rudolf Steiner's addresses revealed the depth of his insight into the circumstances of each individual's incarnation, that person's soul character and spirit aspirations under the unique constraints and conditions of destiny.

In one of his memorial addresses it was recorded that Steiner said of a theosophist's completed soul work, "Quite possibly, this can be appreciated only by those who were as close to her soul as I was."[53] And after the death of one member, he said:

It is such a pleasure to encounter a nature such as hers in life. Those who knew her will have a deep sense of how intimately Miss Schmidt's soul was connected to spiritual activity. Her closest associates have lost much with the passing of this soul, who was as open to the spiritual life as she was retiring with regard to outer life. Few people knew her because she was seldom outgoing, but those who did know her will understand what I mean by these words.[54]

Often, as in this instance, Rudolf Steiner's words actually revealed very little. Nonetheless, the deceased's path of soul and spirit in the context of this incarnation, the person's path to anthroposophy and its spiritual community, was clearly alive in his consciousness.

In many cases, Rudolf Steiner's descriptions and recollections of deceased members extended to the end of their life, to their final illness. In his memorial addresses, Steiner often referred to conversations with and impressions of people he visited on their sickbeds, even on his busiest days, such as during the Christmas Conference of the Anthroposophical Society 1923/24, when he personally attended to the Norwegian anthroposophist Georga Wiese.[55] He spoke repeatedly of impressions individuals made on him in their last days of life or even on their deathbeds, as was the case with the sculptor Jacques de Jaager.[56] Whether his descriptions were phenomenological or symptomatic, they always reflected the depth of the person's completed life and spiritual path.

When Rudolf Steiner had to bid premature farewells to his best and most capable co-workers, his shock was quite visible in his announcements to the members and, later, in his memorial addresses. Nonetheless, he spoke with certainty of how the deceased would continue to work after crossing the threshold. Steiner's addresses always revealed tremendous gratitude for earthly encounters with the deceased, for their individual contributions to the work of anthroposophy, and for their earthly existence as a whole:

When confronted with death we sense for the first time the blessing bestowed on us by the wise leadership of cosmic existence in bringing us together with one or the other person whom karma lovingly guided toward us.[57]

At the end of each memorial address, Rudolf Steiner asked the assembled anthroposophists to rise as a token of their connection to the individuality of the deceased: *"Let us now rise from our seats as a sign that we are uniting with her."*[58] Here, too, Rudolf Steiner used the spiritual "we" form.

*

2

Interment Addresses

At moments such as this, we are especially likely to think about what it means to speak with the sense of responsibility that derives from knowing not only that a spiritual world exists in general but also that on a concrete level, someone is looking down on you, someone who once worked with you here in efforts to confirm the existence and nature of spiritual worlds.[59]

AT INTERMENTS, the "end of the earthly path," Rudolf Steiner spoke after the ritual conducted by the priest. According to Steiner, it was up to the priest with his "words of consecration" to perform the tangible ritual act of guiding the soul of the deceased over into the realm of spirit.[60]

Following the ritual, Rudolf Steiner spoke, if asked to do so by relatives and friends, as an "interpreter" of the priest's words.[61] At the same time, he expressed the "feelings of the spiritual community" to which the deceased belonged.[62] What this means, however, is that Rudolf Steiner spoke on behalf of the anthroposophical movement. He spoke for "our community."[63] He was the community's "spokesperson" in both the earthly and spiritual worlds; this community of spirit spoke "through" him.[64] It was in this sense that Rudolf Steiner began his address at the cremation of the painter Hermann Linde on June 29, 1923:

> Now that priestly words have accompanied our dear friend into the realm of light, it is time for the hearts of those most closely connected to him to speak to his dear wife and daughters and also to you, dear friends, who were so closely associated with Hermann Linde. Although these words are addressed to you, may they also ring out toward the soul of our precious friend.[65]

*

Like his recollections of the dead in other contexts, Rudolf Steiner's interment addresses deal with the soul-spirit being of the deceased, the particular path in earthly existence, and the signature of each unique and irrecoverable life. The community of mourners came together in sharing this view of the deceased's being and path.

Rudolf Steiner's words were wrested from (and always related to) pain: "My dear friends, it cannot be the purpose of spiritual science to ease the pain that settles over our souls when we experience great loss, for pain is a cosmic principle."[66] To also feel and help to bear the pain of the deceased's close relatives, Steiner maintained, should be a deep concern—a promise, even—of the community of anthroposophical friends. Not at Hermann Linde's cremation, but at the beginning of a lecture that same evening in the *Schreinerei* (carpenters' workshop) in Dornach, Steiner said:

> He left his beloved wife and dear daughters behind for our community. In true inner warmth of heart, we must understand how to help these dear friends bear the pain of his passing. For the duration of our time on earth, we must understand how to make our thoughts of him truly valuable by preserving our bonds of love to these friends whom he left behind. This must be our will, and it will become his spiritual joy. Our connection to those he left behind can become a source of satisfaction to his spirit and soul as he looks down on this place where he was active for so long.[67]

According to Steiner, the anthroposophical community can and will relate to surviving relatives in this way, taking into account the deceased's individuality and further journey in the spiritual world. In this way, spiritual community-building would become a real and active force.

In the evening after the burial of the young wife of a man working on the Dornach building, Rudolf Steiner described the particular circumstances of her early death and the spiritual experiences that accompanied it. He then said:

> I wanted to emphasize this thought, my dear friends, both because it can be uplifting for the many friends who attended the burial this afternoon and because it serves as a starting

point for you who will welcome Mr. Schleutermann back into your ranks when he returns to work here after his grief has eased somewhat. The strength that flows toward him from your thoughts can be a comfort to him, just as he will find a great deal of uplifting strength in the beautiful, supersensibly oriented thoughts that were his late wife's last thoughts in this earthly incarnation.

And now, my dear friends, let me ask you to rise from your seats as a sign of our intention to stand by our friend in his great sorrow.[68]

*

Rudolf Steiner intention was that the anthroposophical community assembled in Dornach should know the deceased members, continue to learn from them, and remain connected to them. Steiner described the freely willed promise to do so as a "solemn vow." Addressing the deceased, Rudolf Steiner said in one interment address:

> From the words of our solemn vow here today, we will draw strength, that our thoughts of you may always seek you and that you may always find this community in all worlds inhabited by human souls through all transformations of existence, in cosmic distances and through all expanses of time. We pledge this faithfully to you today, together with your precious relatives and closest friends, for all times to come.[69]

*

The first signs of this direct and emphatic turning to the deceased were evident in Rudolf Steiner's address for Caroline von Sivers.[70] It then appeared for the first time in a stenographic transcript in December 1914, on the occasion of the burial of Albrecht Faiss, the father of little Theo Faiss.[71] Two months later, in February 1915, Rudolf Steiner spoke directly to the deceased, exclusively in the "you" form, at the interment of Fritz Mitscher.[72] Shortly before, at the earthly farewells for the anthroposophist Lina Grosheintz on January 10, 1915, Rudolf Steiner used for the first time a verse he wrote himself for an interment:

> Let us attempt to feel, to perceive, to research what lives in this soul when we imagine her free of all earthly heaviness and earthly sheaths. If we could hear her, what would she say out of her deepest conviction, her deepest feeling and willing? Dear mourners, we might hear this strength-filled soul speak these words:

Into cosmic distances I will carry
My feeling heart—so that it grows warm
In the fire of the holy forces' working;

Into cosmic thoughts I will weave
My own thinking—so that it grows clear
In the light of eternal life-becoming;

Into depths of soul I will sink
Devoted contemplation—so that it grows strong
For human work's true aims.

In the peace of God I strive
Amidst life's battles and cares
To prepare my self for the higher Self;

Aspiring to work in joy-filled peace,
Sensing cosmic being in my own being,
I seek to fulfill my human obligation;

May I thus live in anticipation—
Turned toward my destiny's star—
Which gives me my place in spirit realms.

Rudolf Steiner then explained:

> My dear friends, her soul was so thoroughly imbued with this spirit, so alive with longing for the light that speaks from spiritual worlds, that when I attempted this morning to feel at one with her as her soul hastens toward the spiritual world, I could hear the words she was speaking as she follows her Self's purest impulse, which radiated from her life's star as long as she dwelt among us.
>
> May these words become conscious in our hearts. To me, they seem as if spoken by the soul that is hastening away as we linger for these last moments by her earthly remains. She calls to us, exhorts us, concerned about our path. From the spiritual world, she calls out these words that will give us the strength to feel united with her and to find the way into that world. It is as if her soul were speaking to us in these words, which we must carry with us faithfully in constant remembrance of her.[73]

This is Rudolf Steiner's account of how he received the verse he wrote down and recited for Lina Grosheintz, as if *"spoken by the soul that is hastening away as we linger for these last moments by her earthly remains. She calls to us, exhorts us, concerned about our path. From the spiritual world she calls out these words...."* Steiner formulated this verse to connect with the deceased and to accompany her into the spiritual world: *"words that will give us the strength to feel united with her and to find the way into that world."* He hints at how the verse came about on the morning of the cremation: *"When I attempted... to feel at one with her as her soul hastens toward the spiritual world, I could hear the words...."*

Five weeks later, Rudolf Steiner spoke in greater detail about his experience on the morning of Lina Grosheintz's cremation. In a lecture, he spoke about the deceased's existence at the time when the verse was written down:

Even before the cremation, the need was evident to perceive what this personality would have to say after death, when her remaining connection to her etheric body still permitted some measure of earthly communication. This communication, however, encompassed everything interwoven with her soul through her intensive experience with the anthroposophical worldview. This was a personality who lived to be quite old and who, in her final years, found a home for all of her heart forces in our spiritual scientific worldview.

Then she passed through the portal of death. Before the cremation, her etheric body was still available to her as a means of expression; she could still express herself in earthly words because her etheric body was still there to experience them. At the same time, however, her new freedom from the body and from earthly existence made it possible for her to sum up everything that had been inscribed on her soul through her heart.

On the second day after her death, it became evident that this personality who had passed through the portal of death was attempting to express her inmost nature, and this expression took the form of the words I have shared with you, which must therefore be seen as words experienced by the deceased. We must imagine that on the second day after passing through the portal of death, this being's soul was filled with (and spoke through) the force of these words.

Putting ourselves in the deceased soul's place allowed her being to speak through us in these words. At the cremation, therefore, I could do no better than to speak these words to the deceased; in effect, she herself was speaking them to the friends gathered around her earthly remains. I can assure you, I added nothing, absolutely nothing; I simply tried to record these words as they emerged from the being of the deceased.[74]

In Wellenweiten will ich tragen
Mein fühlend Herz, dass warm es werde
Im Feuer heil'gen Kräftewirkens;

In Weltgedanken will ich weben
Das eigne Denken, dass klar es werde
Im Licht des ew'gen Werde-Lebens;

In Seelengründe will ich tauchen
Ergeb'nes Sinnen, dass stark es werde
Für Menschenwirkens wahre Ziele;

In Gottes Ruhe streb' ich so
Mit Lebenskämpfen und mit Sorgen,
Mein Selbst zum höhern Selbst bereitend;

Nach arbeitfreud'gem Frieden trachtend,
Erahnend Welten-Sein im Eigensein,
möcht' ich die Menschenpflicht erfüllen;

Erwartend leben darf ich dann
Entgegen meinem Schicksalsterne,
Der mir im Geistgebiet den Ort erteilt.

4: Verse from Rudolf Steiner for Lina Grosheintz (1915)

Intense involvement with anthroposophical contents had so completely occupied the years before Lina Grosheintz's earthly death that the process of absorbing and internalizing spiritual science not only produced "life forces" in her soul but became an essential component of her soul existence: "These years of immersing herself in the spiritual-scientific worldview became intrinsic to her soul itself"—a process that came to expression in the verse uttered by Rudolf Steiner, a verse that "spoke itself."[75] The words emerged from the soul of the deceased, resounded from her being. Rudolf Steiner emphasized repeatedly that they belonged not to him but to the deceased. As such, they were a "self-description in the first person."[76] (*Sensing cosmic being in my own being....*)

In mid March 1915, two months after Lina Grosheintz's cremation, Rudolf Steiner explained the entire process again in a lecture in Nuremberg:

> What happened in the case of this personality? Very shortly after her death, when her soul had cast off the physical body but was still united with the etheric body and experiencing the etheric tableau of her life, it was as if the Self that her soul was then attempting to grasp flowed outward. At that point, I simply wrote down these words. They were not shaped by my human knowledge. They are a summary, of sorts, of what she had received from spiritual science, and they reflect the workings of her soul in her efforts to achieve full inner self-awareness.[77]

During the etheric life tableau, the deceased soul was attempting to come to grips with the body-free state and to reorient its consciousness to the spiritual world. This process of achieving "full inner self-awareness" drew on the substance of anthroposophy—that is, on the soul's actual journey and experiences in life and the anthroposophical contents she had received. Rudolf Steiner identified with the deceased's actual being, with her soul's situation after death, and put himself in her place: "Here the observing soul has nothing to do but insert itself fully into the other soul, which is still applying the etheric body's forces in the effort to come to grips with its essence, enriched by spiritual science, in order to clarify how to orient itself now in the spiritual world."[78] Rudolf Steiner reflected this process in earthly words. The verse he spoke at the cremation was not arbitrary; he was listening to "the divine voice that bids us do what we must do."[79] His address (and especially the mantric verse) was intended to help the deceased on her way—to help her achieve new I-consciousness in the spiritual world.[80] During the cremation address, Rudolf Steiner already experienced the real effects of this support:

> It was quite obviously helpful to the deceased when those left behind in physical bodies assisted her in putting into words what was happening in her soul.[81]

*

Two weeks after Lina Grosheintz's funeral, at the cremation of the anthroposophist Sibyl Colazza in Zurich in late January of 1915, Rudolf Steiner again addressed a verse to the deceased: *"May these words, which arose in my thinking through the thinking of your spirit, be spoken through and out of the inmost aspect of my soul."*[82] At the end of his address, Steiner repeated the verse after these words of explanation: *"Out of this deeply moved soul, out of a sense of union in soul-spirit striving, may these words be spoken to you and received by your spirit hearing. May they find their way into your soul to re-enliven its image as it appeared during your earthly activity."*[83]

Later Rudolf Steiner said that as he turned in thought toward the deceased a few days after her death, the words of the verse for Sibyl Colazza emerged from her spirit's thinking and appeared in his own:

Identifying with the inner being of our friend who departed in midlife, submerging our thinking in the deceased's soul and allowing its contents to flow into our own thoughts, makes it possible to say how this soul was in life and how she is now, after death. This is how she appeared in the days before her cremation, after completing the review of her life through the etheric body.[84]

In a different lecture, Steiner again spoke about the circumstances surrounding the emergence of the verse for Sibyl Colazza, which had formed the center of his interment address in Zurich:

These words really had very little to do with my own ability to formulate such things. Instead, they resulted from identifying with the soul of the personality who had passed through the portal of death. They arose from the need to characterize her soul in a way that she herself inspired or illuminated. It was as if her soul said to me, formulate words that will resound with what is characteristic of my soul. Since her soul was still in an unconscious state, however, those words did not emerge from consciousness but rather from her essential nature. These words characterize her, not as if in any egotistical reflection, but as she appeared to herself when observed by another soul.[85]

Speaking of Lina Grosheintz's interment, Rudolf Steiner had indicated very briefly that the words he spoke in verse form held significance for the deceased: "It was quite obviously helpful to the deceased when those left behind in physical bodies assisted her in putting into words what was happening in her soul." Steiner describes Sibyl Colazza's situation during the address and subsequent cremation in somewhat more detail:

Our friend had passed the stage of the etheric review, so we were speaking to a present but not conscious being. Then heat triggered a moment of consciousness and she watched the cremation.[86]

Elsewhere, Steiner says more about the condition of the deceased Sibyl Colazza's consciousness at the time of cremation:

> Now in fact this soul had been as if she were asleep during the funeral ceremony. Then the cremation followed. Strangely enough, her first moment of consciousness, which then faded again, occurred as heat (if not actual flames) engulfed the corpse. This impression of heat was accompanied by the first flash of real consciousness in our friend's soul. The entire funeral ceremony then appeared to her soul in retrospect, *that is, she perceived what had been spoken.*[87]

In a third account, Rudolf Steiner describes the entire process—his address, the verse, the cremation, and the deceased's consciousness—as follows:

> The cremation speech had been given, framed by these words [of the verse]. As the body was engulfed in flames—or at least, what looked like flames, although it was actually only ascending heat—her soul experienced a moment of awakening. One could see how her soul looked back on the whole scene that had taken place among the people gathered for the cremation and especially on what had been said. Then, of course, her soul began to sink back down into a superabundance of consciousness or, as we would say, into unconsciousness. Later there was another perceptible moment of looking back. These conscious moments last a little longer each time until, finally, complete reorientation to this superabundance of consciousness is achieved.
>
> It is important to note here that because words were spoken at the cremation that came from her own soul, these

words had an awakening effect and kindled consciousness in retrospect in her.[88]

According to Rudolf Steiner, the words that had sounded from Sibyl Colazza's soul (*"which arose in my thinking through the thinking of your spirit"*) supported the process of reconfiguring the deceased's consciousness, "like a first momentary flaring of consciousness."[89]

*

In a slightly different account, Rudolf Steiner reported receiving a "response" from the deceased during the night after giving the cremation address for another anthroposophical friend, young Fritz Mitscher. In February of 1915, Steiner had formulated a verse for Mitscher, which he recited as part of his cremation address. Rudolf Steiner said of this verse that it expressed "what my own soul felt in turning to the soul that had just passed through the portal of death."[90] The verse was formulated and spoken "in community" with the soul of the deceased friend rather than "out of" that soul, as had been the case with Lina Grosheintz only weeks earlier. It was "stimulated in my own soul at the sight of the deceased whose soul was still united with his etheric body."[91]

Rudolf Steiner said that when he reflected on "the impression the deceased made," he did so not only "out of the being of the deceased" but also out of his own soul; the words of the verse had been formulated "in living interaction with the soul who had passed through death."[92] Rudolf Steiner then emphasized again:

> Words like these are spoken in such a way that my own soul simply records them without having much to do with them. They come from the soul of the other; they are written as the result of orienting my soul toward that other soul.[93]

Rudolf Steiner reported that in the night following Fritz Mitscher's cremation, he heard a transformed version of the verse "as if emanating from the being of the deceased" even though the deceased "had certainly not yet achieved orientation" and the I-consciousness he was to discover in the spiritual world.[94] Nonetheless, the words were transformed: *"Everything directed at you came to me; all that was yours came back to me, transformed as if spoken by your soul about its own being."*[95] Many months later, Rudolf Steiner said that he heard these words "resounding as if from the being of the deceased" in a dialogue or communication with the departed.

Rudolf Steiner's lengthy verse for Fritz Mitscher had included these words:

> You nurtured your beautiful gifts
> In order to tread with steady steps
> Bright paths of spirit-knowledge
> As truth's true servant
> Unperturbed by worldly contradiction.

> You trained your spirit-organs
> Which, steadfastly and bravely,
> Pushed aside error for you
> On both sides of your path
> And made a space for truth for you.

> For you, to form your Self
> For the revelation of pure light
> So that the soul's sun-power
> Might shine mightily within you
> Was your life's concern and joy.

> Other cares, other joys
> Barely touched your soul,
> For knowledge seemed to you to be

The light that gives existence meaning,
Seemed to you to be life's true value.

In the "response" from the deceased in the night after the cremation—and also in the months that followed—Rudolf Steiner then heard the words:

To form my Self
To reveal pure light
So that the soul's sun power
Might shine mightily within me
Was my life's concern and joy.

Other cares, other joys
Barely touched my soul,
For knowledge,
As the light that gives existence meaning,
Seemed to me life's true value.[96]

*

Rudolf Steiner's interment addresses, which often culminated in such verses for and to the deceased, generated ongoing connections. As aids on the journey after death, they served the development of new I-consciousness. Simultaneously, however, they enabled the anthroposophical community to remain in connection with the individuality, the spirit-soul, who had left earthly existence.

For the sake of both the deceased and friends remaining behind on earth, Rudolf Steiner attempted to create a true image of the deceased in each address. At the interment of the Norwegian anthroposophist Harald Lille on October 25, 1920, Steiner began with the words:

Dear friend Lille, in the time since your soul left this body, all of the moments in which I was privileged to know you have reappeared to my mind's eye. These memories brought me the image of your being. This image now stands before my soul and the souls of the mourners here, who look up to your soul hastening into the spiritual world as we take leave of you on the physical plane. May what stands before our souls convey your image to this community of mourners.[97]

Rudolf Steiner's entire address, which depicted the soul existence and soul journey of the deceased's completed earthly incarnation, and especially the verse, which both heightened and shaped the description, were intended to allow the essential image of the deceased to appear. Rudolf Steiner said that this "image," actually created by the deceased, now had to be recreated to make possible lasting connections to and union with the departed soul. The presence of this true "image" of the deceased in the souls of those still on earth not only made it possible to find the deceased in the spiritual world but also facilitated his concrete future activity on earth. The recreated "image," said Rudolf Steiner, becomes a force, an organ of the spiritual world through which the deceased is able to initiate connections and contribute to shaping earthly events.

*

5: Johannesbau, February 1914

3

The Goetheanum
and Deceased Co-workers

In the most potent sense of the word, the Goetheanum
needed co-workers—co-workers who would contribute their
greatest ability but also sacrifice their greatest ability.[98]

Rudolf Steiner once called the "Johannesbau"—later known as the first Goetheanum—*"the building of the anthroposophical cause."*[99] Above and beyond the fact that numerous anthroposophists from many nations worked together on the project, the building was an expression of anthroposophy as such, of its being, its content, and its sociality—in short, of "our community." In both inner and outer respects, it was a "building for the anthroposophical cause," the central creation of the spiritual community.

Several individualities close to Rudolf Steiner devoted all of their strength to the building in Dornach and died either as it was being built or as part of the process of its destruction. These early deaths, memorialized by Rudolf Steiner in central addresses, included in particular Theo Faiss, Sophie Stinde, Hermann Linde, and Edith Maryon.

Theo Faiss died in Dornach on October 7, 1914, at age seven, slightly more than a year after the laying of the Johannesbau's foundation stone. Theo was the eldest child of parents who had moved from Stuttgart to Dornach to develop a market garden. After Theo's death, Rudolf Steiner described him as a "very spiritually alert child...with quite exceptional heart-qualities."[100] He was *"a real sun-child"*—"even if you spotted him only briefly here and there, his soul drew your heartfelt attention."[101] When Rudolf Steiner returned to Dornach from a trip to Stuttgart a few days before the child's death, Theo Faiss greeted him on the hill at Dornach: "The boy came toward me in front of the building and held out his hand."[102] The boy's father was away fighting in the war, and Theo tried to take his place, helping his mother in every way possible. He was running an errand in the cafeteria when he died in a tragic accident—a furniture wagon tipped over on him right next to the building.

Rudolf Steiner spoke repeatedly about the detailed circumstances of Theo's death—the routes taken by the wagon and by the boy, each determined by numerous factors that brought Theo to the spot at the exact moment when the wagon tipped over. In several different lectures, Rudolf Steiner dealt with the "remarkable chain of events" that allowed the accident to happen.[103] According to Steiner, these circumstances were all directed by "the boy's karma."[104] *"In this case the boy was only intended to live to age seven in this incarnation."*[105] "If we investigate this incident on a spiritual level, in its karmic connections, we find that the boy's soul summoned the wagon so that he might meet his death at that moment. Everything was arranged."[106] "The furniture wagon was driven there because of the child. The spiritual beings at work behind this mystery arranged everything so the boy could meet his death."[107]

After his lecture, around 10 p.m. on the day of Theo's death, Rudolf Steiner was informed that the boy was missing; the body was recovered around midnight.

Steiner showed a great deal of concern for the boy's mother and siblings:

> In the days between the child's death and burial, Rudolf Steiner came to his mother's house twice a day. The youngest child, less than a year old, was suffering from an ulcerous skin infection and was very uncomfortable. At times the restless, feverish, whimpering baby suddenly grew still in our arms, his face lighted up, and his little head turned toward the door. A few minutes later, Rudolf Steiner invariably appeared, entering quickly from the yard. You should have seen his gesture as he took the baby in his arms, watched his hands as he dabbed and cleaned the raw, inflamed spots with damp cotton. (Fresh chamomile infusion always had to be prepared to his exact specifications, and it had to be just the right temperature.) The baby always looked at him intently with big eyes, his little

6: Theo Faiss, three years old

face relaxed in a silent smile, and he always fell into a long, restful sleep as soon as his healer left.[108]

*

When Theo's body was laid out, Rudolf Steiner visited daily. On October 10, 1914, he gave the interment address. That same evening in the *Schreinerei*, he spoke about the death of the child "whose body we entrusted to Mother Earth today."[109] Steiner concluded with these sentences:

> When we are certain that the soul has left its bodily sheaths, we speak the mantra that most of the friends here already know. This verse, with slight alterations, is the one I will now send to our dear, good Theo, whose soul now dwells in spheres beyond:
>
>> Spirit of his soul, active guardian,
>> May your wings carry
>> Our souls' entreating love
>> To the humans in the spheres entrusted to your care
>> So that, united with your power,
>> Our pleas may stream with aid
>> For the soul they seek in love.[110]

Already in a talk in the *Schreinerei* on October 10, 1914, three days after the boy's death, Rudolf Steiner pointed to forces that emanate from the being of one who dies young, to the benefit of earthly affairs: "When a human life ends early, when a human soul's time of learning is cut short, forces that would otherwise have been applied to the physical body stream down from the spiritual world and continue to work."[111] Rudolf Steiner returned to this subject with ever-increasing emphasis in the following months, explaining that the human body of formative forces includes a will element or element of creative love.[112] This element unites with knowledge about the formative principles of the human body, about its "building" or structure.[113] The etheric body itself is cosmic in nature; at birth, it shines with macrocosmic imaginations and reflects the cosmos, the cosmic forces and cosmic light of heaven.[114] When this body of formative forces, instead of being used to complete a long earthly life, is destined to be released from the physical body through premature death, it is "sacrificed" and available for other purposes after death.

Steiner describes the etheric body of the boy Theo Faiss as "truly filled with forces of the Eternal and Good."[115] Soon after Theo's death, his individuality adapted this etheric body and applied it to aiding the construction process in Dornach. In early 1915, three months after Theo's death, Rudolf Steiner reported that the building's entire "aura" had changed. Theo's body of formative forces, released by his individuality and greatly expanded, had merged its forces with the building's aura, where it was now active: "The forces are there; anyone who sees them, anyone who can see them, recognizes that they have passed over into the aura of our building in Dornach and are alive within it."[116] *"Here in this building, we ourselves are living within the aura of an etheric body."*[117] This etheric aura, said Steiner, hovered around the building, enclosing and enlivening it: "It is quite possible to determine the boundaries of this enclosure."[118] For the first and only time, Rudolf Steiner drew the geographical limits of the "enclosure" on a chalkboard during his lecture of June 13, 1915, to members of the Anthroposophical Society in Elberfeld bei Wuppertal. Describing the topographical situation in Dornach, he said:

> This building here is the boiler house, designed specifically according to spiritual scientific principles, and here we have another building where the glass windows for the building are being engraved. Let me also mention in passing that the house called Villa Hansi, where we live, is here.

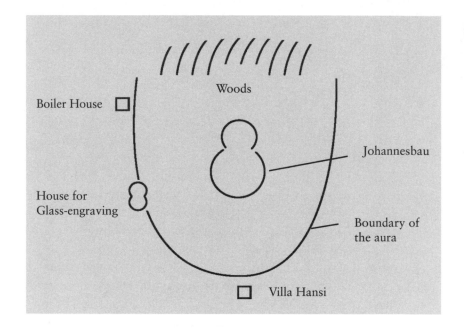

7: Drawing from GA 159, page 282.

Strangely enough, the aura of little Theodor Faiss extends from the woods up here, passes by the boiler house, cuts through the middle of the window workshop, and then also passes by Villa Hansi. As you see, it surrounds the entire building, so when we enter the building, we are walking into this etheric aura.[119]

Rudolf Steiner spoke repeatedly about the concrete significance of this transformed "etheric aura" for the ongoing work on the Johannesbau: "Anyone who has had (or has yet to have) anything to do with our building in Dornach since that afternoon in late fall when little Theo passed through the portal of death will recognize changes in the building's spiritual aura as a result of the incorporation of Theo's etheric body."[120] According to Rudolf Steiner, these new forces at work in the building's surroundings offered support to those who needed *"to find ideas for the building that would integrate it into the spiritual world in the right way."* [121] "If you yourself work on behalf of the Anthroposophical Society's building in Dornach, if you are involved in initiating what happens there, you are aware of what we owe to the helping forces that work into our souls from such an aura."[122] Forces from the etheric body of the deceased Theo Faiss, said Steiner, stimulated artistic ideas and impulses; the "structural force" of that body of formative forces made possible or supported inspirations regarding the building's further development. "We gain access to the most beautiful forces inspiring what is being created [in Dornach] by uniting our own souls with the expansion [of this etheric body], which has expanded, become like a miniature world, and is now alive in the atmosphere surrounding the building."[123] *"Turning our own souls toward the etheric body of little Theo, which is active in the atmosphere around the building,"* gives access to "forces that transmit" the necessary inspirations and intuitions. "We feel these forces within us, just as we sense the building in our souls."[124] On June 13, 1915, Rudolf Steiner explained further:

While it is true that all the forces in the young etheric body of little Theodor Faiss would otherwise still be present in the spiritual world, pulling them all together would be a Herculean task. That situation changes because they came together through the boy, making it significantly easier to be inspired by them.[125]

*

According to Rudolf Steiner, the path Theo Faiss took was a path of sacrifice orchestrated by the spiritual world: "A family moves into the neighborhood of the building. This family has a child whose soul-nature is especially gifted, and he sacrifices his etheric body to envelop the building in its forces."[126] The child's body of formative forces is a "gift from the spiritual world."[127] Its power protects the building: "There is something wonderfully powerful at work in such a connection."[128] Rudolf Steiner made no further statements about the individuality and destiny of Theo Faiss, indicating only that in the broader context, Theo's sacrificial deed was to be seen as a great spiritual act:

> It would take us too far afield to go into the actual karma of a human soul capable of such sacrifice, which cannot be brought about artificially. It must be related to the person's entire karma. Such a person is called to do something that plays a role in the spiritual, cosmic development of humanity, for example, on behalf of this building of ours in Dornach, which will house our spiritual-scientific endeavors.[129]

*

SOPHIE STINDE, one of Rudolf Steiner's most important co-workers, whom he once described as the "soul" of the Dornach building, died thirteen months after Theo Faiss. Born into a North German pastor's family, Stinde had been a landscape

Die Bewegung ist der Impuls des Willens
Die Sinne _____ die Impulse des
Gedankens.

Tod = er giebt als befruchtenden Keim für die
Fortentwicklung den menschl. Astralleib ab —
Ohne diesen enthält die Welt nur die
toten Producte der Vorwelt —
Wenn aber keine spir. Gedanken
abgegeben würden, dann geht die
Welt der Finsternis entgegen —
Es sind dies die Sonnenkeime ▪

8: Undated notebook entry by Rudolf Steiner

painter. Beginning in 1902, she developed and led the Munich branch of the Theosophical Society, including its esoteric work. Together with her friend Countess Pauline von Kalckreuth, she initiated the activity of the Munich center and made possible both the Whitsun conference of 1907 and the Mystery Dramas of 1910 to 1913. As the first chairperson of the Johannesbau-Verein (Johannes Building Association), she played a central role in planning the building and making it a reality. She died unexpectedly in Munich on the evening of November 17, 1915, at age sixty-two. Rudolf Steiner attributed her death to exhaustion of life forces due to the excess of work she accomplished on behalf of the Anthroposophical Society's building: "We saw with trepidation the fatigue of the frequently overtaxed physical body through which her soul manifested."[130]

Rudolf Steiner was close to Sophie Stinde, acknowledged his indebtedness to her, and considered here one of "our very, very best workers."[131] On November 18, he conveyed the news of her death to members of the Anthroposophical Society in Berlin, where he was staying at the time. He spoke at her cremation in Ulm four days later (November 22) and held lectures in her memory in Munich (November 29) as well as in Dornach (December 26), although the funeral service had already taken place there soon after her death: "My dear friends, I cannot resume these lectures here without commemorating the departure of Sophie Stinde's soul from the physical plane. Her passing has made a deep incision in our life."[132]

Conscious of her enduring connection to the building under construction and with the goal of facilitating the members' ongoing relationship to Stinde's individuality, Rudolf Steiner again held a memorial address in the *Schreinerei* in Dornach on the anniversary of her death on November 18, 1916. The building in Dornach, said Steiner, was "born out of Sophie Stinde's soul."[133] This statement, applied "not only to [the building's] purpose but also to the force of love indispensable to its coming about, as well as to the artistic sensibility without which no world-view can pour itself out into art."[134] Sophie Stinde was "among those most intimately" connected to the building and had been "one of the first" to conceive of the idea.[135] In his memorial address of December 16, 1915, five weeks after her death, Rudolf Steiner had said:

> That we were in a position to implement the idea of the building, which was originally intended to be constructed in Munich and is now going up in Dornach, is intimately related to Sophie Stinde's hopes for our work. She is largely responsible for the first germ of the idea of this building. That first germinal idea was bound up with her aspirations and hopes for our spiritual work and was the beneficiary of her dedicated activity, as were all other aspects of our work.[136]

Referring to his work with Sophie Stinde, Rudolf Steiner had emphasized:

> "We worked alongside her in Dornach; we watched as the artistic forms that would envelop our work unfolded bit by bit in our building in there. It was precious and dear to us to work with her on this building and watch how it gradually developed.[137]

*

In his addresses after Sophie Stinde's death as well as at her cremation, Rudolf Steiner described her early connection to anthroposophy. Her presence and commitment had made it possible for him to begin lecturing on spiritual science in Munich as early as 1904, and her apartment was the venue for "the first members-only lectures on these matters that I held in Munich."[138] Describing the larger context of these beginnings in Munich, Rudolf Steiner said, "That was only a short time after

9: Johannesbau, March 1914

we began our work in Central Europe, and we were trying to find homes for this work in various places."[139] In this connection, Rudolf Steiner spoke on December 26, 1916, about the main prerequisites of anthroposophical activity and the need for the Anthroposophical Society to exist, emphasizing:

> We must distinguish two factors here. The first is the content of our work, which must be derived from the spiritual world. If the earth is to achieve its goal, this content must stream into humanity's spiritual evolution in future earthly times. Our souls must face this fact with all due humility. At present, we may either be convinced of the truth of this content or reject it, but even if our present efforts falter because of the resistance of souls too weak for our cause, this content will have to stream into humanity's spiritual evolution, perhaps already now but certainly eventually.
>
> A quite different matter is our society's internal work in the circle attempting to incorporate our worldview's spiritual content into humanity's culture—that is, to bring this content to the souls and hearts of individuals who need it. In this instance, we cannot say, well, if not now, then later. We have only one chance to apply ourselves whole-heartedly, with undivided souls. We all know individuals who apply themselves in this way, placing all their assets and abilities in the service of our cause as if this work were the most necessary task incumbent upon them in this life. We can say that these individuals grasp the full meaning and significance of how our work is meant to flow into world spiritual culture through a circle of people organized into a society.
>
> In the first instance, with regard to the content of our worldview, no individual goodwill is required, only the inherent truth of the matter. (We must, however, acknowledge the possibility of failure; perhaps the time when this content will be incorporated into humanity's spiritual

culture lies in the more distant future.) There, understanding the content and learning to perceive its truth is all that
counts. There is no need to talk about trust or ways of
developing our will; we need to speak only of the inherent
truth of the matter.

It is different when we consider the instrument intended
to guide the spiritual content of our worldview into the
world. This instrument has nothing to do with the truth of
the content. For this truth to flow as it must into present
developments, however, mutual trust among members is
required, as is their goodwill, the goodwill that unites with
the warmth and light of our cause.

With regard to working in a specific place, there are
several further considerations. First, individuals called to
specific work have the goodwill to contribute everything
given to them by karma up to the moment they enter our
spiritual house, so to speak, through the portal of our spiritual endeavors. Second, they understand how to transform
all their gifts in this incarnation to serve our cause. People
come with different gifts and abilities, but even if they start
from opposite points on the periphery, there are no paths
in life that cannot lead to the center, to the gateway into
this house. *Miss Stinde was like this.*[140]

In Steiner's words, Sophie Stinde possessed "the goodwill that unites with the warmth and light of our cause"; she
stepped through the portal into the "spiritual house," and was
ready to place all of her abilities in the service of anthroposophy. *"She belonged to those who took up our cause in the
profoundest depths of her heart and identified with that cause
completely."*[141] She applied not only her complete personality but also her formidable capacity for work to the "cause"
of anthroposophy. She abandoned her art and made herself
completely available to her new profession, recognizing and
living out its Christian essence.

In his cremation address, Rudolf Steiner said:

> Inherent in all of her spiritual aptitudes was a search for the inner path that leads to connection with the Christ, who touches not only the deepest human feelings but also the highest human thoughts. For our dear friend, the Christ was alive. She could perceive the Christ-Impulse in every detail of everything human work and human energy accomplish in earthly evolution. In her searching, she found the living Christ; he lives in all, but as an individual being he can be discovered only through the most profound spiritual exertion. So there she stood, uniting her striving for the Christ with our striving, a joy to us who worked alongside her. She came to join us; for the sake of our work, she laid down the daily work she had been doing with such great hope.[142]

Rudolf Steiner spoke in the plural—"*our* striving," "*our* work"—on behalf of the anthroposophical movement and as its principal earthly representative. In 1904, Sophie Stinde had joined forces with him and with the work and teachings he represented, to Rudolf Steiner's great pleasure: "a joy to us who worked alongside her."[143] Her commitment to the developing anthroposophical work was absolute: "She devoted [her] life's best forces to the needs of our work, accepting any sacrifice it required as a matter of course."[144]

Steiner called Sophie Stinde a "nobly formed" artistic nature.[145] She brought her artistic energies to anthroposophical work through the gateway of its "spiritual house." Her landscape paintings were dominated by "the loveliest grasp of nature, the most intimate interaction with the spirit that pervades and enlivens nature."[146] Sophie Stinde united these subtle artistic and spiritual forces with anthroposophy's earthly development, as Rudolf Steiner described on November 29, 1915, in Munich, where she had worked for so many years:

We sense the direction of Sophie Stinde's strength in how her soul-deeds flowed into our spiritual work. That strength, full of artistic sensibility and warmth, poured artistic imagination into what the spirit is attempting to develop in our midst. If those most deeply connected to our work have any access at all to what art carries and fosters, they will value what it means for our spiritual-scientific work when artistic imagination unites with the practical soul-properties this work requires. After all, the colors and forms that flow from the human soul into artistic ways of working are transformed into spiritual-scientific perception in other spheres; in effect, they become the cognitive forces of spiritual science. Those who contribute from realms of art, out of the warmth of their enthusiasm for art, out of the wealth of artistic creativity, enrich our field of activity with infinite treasures.[147]

*

From the beginning, Sophie Stinde had a profound understanding of anthroposophy—not only of the explicit contents of lectures and writings, but also of much that Rudolf Steiner left unspoken. ("And so she appeared among us. From the first moment we met her, she demonstrated her understanding of both the expressed and the unexpressed ways our worldview supports human existence. Few individuals were able to take in all of these spoken and unspoken aspects with an understanding as profound and heartfelt as Sophie Stinde's. Few were as able as she to imbue the contents of our spiritual view with such fire of will and warmth of feeling in conveying them to the hearts of friends."[148]) In this sense, Rudolf Steiner was soon able to rely on Sophie Stinde and entrust her with responsible work. In his memorial address in Munich, Steiner spoke of the confidence and cooperation that develop between individuals who are connected "in the depths of their souls":

10: Sophie Stinde (1853-1915)

When we approach the work of a lifetime, we are often initially uncertain about what to do in specific instances. In such moments, we take the hand of a friend and say, this is how we expect you to help us, to work alongside us on what we intend to do. To certain friends with strong souls, however, we do not need to say this; the connection is so deep that we simply need to tell them what we ourselves know at that beginning stage. They are so intimately related to us and our striving that they will work with us even when the work's fruits and its very nature can become evident only in the course of working together. Below the threshold of consciousness, a loyalty develops that connects these souls for life. This essential loyalty, based on a spiritual striving such as ours is meant to be, binds souls together not only in their manifestations and actions on the physical plane but also even in the profoundest depths of spiritual existence.[149]

Without a doubt, Sophie Stinde was one of those "friends with strong souls" with whom Rudolf Steiner was connected through karma, through the lifelong loyalty that connects souls "even in the profoundest depths of spiritual existence."

*

According to Rudolf Steiner, Sophie Stinde's development of the outreach work of the Anthroposophical Society in Munich was exemplary, selfless, and objective in ways that transcended the personal; that is, her actions were based on the needs of anthroposophy itself: "This vital core of connection and loyalty to one's work signifies a selfless union with that work."[150] "Anyone as closely connected to our work as Sophie Stinde works without regard for personal concerns, on a purely objective basis, for the goals our striving sets for itself."[151] Stinde followed anthroposophy's spiritual concerns on behalf of civilization out of the "inner qualities of her being."[152] She was guided reliably by her "straightforward sense of truth."[153] She acted out of trust and love combined with rigor, precision, and a sense of responsibility. *"She brought joy to our life."*[154]

In its ethos and perception of future tasks, Sophie Stinde's work facilitated the development of both anthroposophy and our building in Dornach, and stood "as an example for us all."[155] *"There is no aspect of this building or of the rest of our spiritual-scientific work that has not been deeply imbued with and supported by Sophie Stinde's spiritual help,"* emphasized Rudolf Steiner in Munich on November 29, 1915.[156] In his address at the cremation in Ulm, he put it like this:

> She worked in such a way that all of her earthly co-workers felt a connection to her. An unforgettable light radiated from her workplace, a light that will illuminate many people for a long time to come. She was so very deeply entrenched in our work that she ultimately sacrificed all of her working energy to it. Even now that she is no longer among us in physical existence, that extremely valuable energy remains palpable in our work. Sophie Stinde's spirit-voice, which we became accustomed to hearing and listened to with profound respect for so many years, will always continue to resound mysteriously from our workplace, from all our working hours, from our very way of working.[157]

In Berlin, speaking on the day after her death, Rudolf Steiner said that Sophie Stinde would continue to support anthroposophical efforts toward a *"spiritual world culture."* In Sophie Stinde, Steiner lost one of his best earthly co-workers, just two years after the laying of the foundation stone for the Johannesbau, which she had attended, and at a time beset with countless difficulties.[158] Nonetheless, in Berlin on November 18, 1915, he said:

As you know, our cause faces many challenges and great opposition in the world. But most especially in Miss Stinde's case, let me emphasize this: Those who pass through the portal of death simply alter the form of their souls' existence. We who truly and honestly pledge our allegiance to the spiritual worlds can count such souls as faithfully united with us. They are our most important and significant co-workers. The veils that often still surround us in our physical embodiments are gradually falling away, and the souls of our precious dead are working among us. We know this to be a fact, and we need their help. We need help that cannot be contested on the physical plane and is no longer affected by obstacles encountered there. In our profound, sincere belief in the progress of our cause in world culture, we are fully conscious that our best workers are those who were once with us and now work among us through spiritual means from the spiritual world. Sometimes we need to reinforce our confidence in our cause by thanking our dead friends for being among us and acknowledging that their forces, united with ours, enable us to accomplish the work incumbent on us on behalf of spiritual world culture.[159]

*

Especially in his addresses in Dornach on December 26, 1915, and November 17, 1916, Rudolf Steiner emphasized the need to relate concretely to Sophie Stinde's individuality, transcending the threshold of death and focusing on the building in Dornach into which she had poured all her spiritual, artistic, social, and organizational energy.[160] In the earlier of these two addresses, Rudolf Steiner said of the deceased:

In the outer, physical world, her place will be empty in future. But for those who learned to understand her, the thought of her exemplary, devoted, self-sacrificing work among us will emanate from that empty place. This thought must be especially alive in the spaces under the double dome, which owed so much to Sophie Stinde's efforts and where her soul was so active during this earthly incarnation. When we take up our relationship with her in the right way, it will be impossible for us to look at these forms without feeling connected to her. Her soul will continue to work there.[161]

Sophie Stinde, said Steiner, was at work in the spaces of the Johannesbau as it developed, *"blessing the building"*; the spirit of her soul would continue to work there *"as the soul of our building."*[162] Rudolf Steiner asked the Dornach co-workers to be conscious of this fact: "May many, many souls understand how Sophie Stinde's soul is united with this spiritual project of ours."[163] In fact, he invited her fellow workers to turn in spirit to Stinde's individuality, directing their questions and concerns to her:

Let me say this, dear friends, to you who valued and loved Sophie Stinde and were united with her in true friendship: Turn your feelings, your thoughts, and your entire loving soul-being toward the spirit places where you sense Sophie Stinde's soul-presence. Make a habit of doing this whenever you need strength for what you must accomplish on earth, whenever you need advice and encouragement for anything you are attempting to do. Turn to her soul in its spirit dwelling, to the soul who so often stood beside you in life, offering advice and active assistance. You will not turn to her in vain. In moments when you would have sought her out in the visible world, send your thoughts and feelings to her place in the spirit. Your soul will then feel intimately connected to her. If you learned to love and value her in the right way in earthly existence, she will turn her spirit's gaze, her soul's eye, and her spirit power to you

and you will experience her advice and help in the depths
of your soul. Sophie Stinde was one of our first workers.
Where she dwells now, having left the physical body, she
will also be one of our most effective spirit workers.[164]

Rudolf Steiner concluded his address of December 26, 1915,
with these sentences:

> My dear friends, in this place that is so pervaded by Sophie
> Stinde's soul, it seems only fitting to begin my address with
> some introductory words of commemoration. Having
> loved her when she walked among us in a physical body,
> we will also love her as we bask in the endless warmth and
> illumination of her spirit. Let us seek her among those to
> whom we look up with special devotion at this time of
> year, when the spirit realms shine even brighter than at
> other seasons. In particular, let us seek those potent forces
> emanating from Sophie Stinde's soul. May we be worthy
> to receive them as they continue to pervade our work,
> especially in these spaces here.[165]

*

In the cremation speech in Ulm on November 22, Rudolf
Steiner had addressed Sophie Stinde's individuality directly, in
these words:

> Yes, we look up to you in pain at the loss of the deep
> blessing that streamed toward us through the many years
> when your being was united with ours. We behold you
> in spirit, and you yourself, with your familiar strength
> and kind, loving manner, are a solace to us. You are our
> solace because we believe we draw from your heart, from
> your deep soul, the promise that your strength will work
> in ours if we continue to work at what we believe to be

Déposé · O Rietmann
N° 67. 8 April 1915

11: Johannesbau, April 1915

right. What you united with us on a temporal basis will
remain united with our souls for all eternity. We can count
on finding you and receiving the blessings of your spirit in
our workplaces, in our work times, and in the energy that
drives our efforts.[166]

Again, Rudolf Steiner had created a cremation verse specifically for Sophie Stinde's *"exemplary soul, which will be an inex-
tinguishable light for us in the spiritual world."*[167] The words
of this verse emerged as he turned toward her being only a few
hours before the cremation: "This image of Sophie Stinde took
shape before my soul as her precious soul drifted away from us
into etheric heights."[168] This verse, too, was intended to unite
the community of mourners gathered in her memory and to
serve as the basis of an effective, lasting, reciprocal relationship:

Today, let us attempt to unite in the image she created
in us through her love, her work, and her energetic and
understanding participation in our efforts. Aware of her
soul's eye looking down on this image, let us attempt to
unite in it. As we recreate the image she herself created
in us, as we recreate it with the right sensibility and love,
and with profound understanding, she will be able to unite
with us.[169]

Rudolf Steiner spoke this verse he had created, the image of
the being of the deceased Sophie Stinde, at the beginning and
end of the cremation address and again in Munich on November
29, 1915:

From earthly being
To spirit's solar land
The beings, whose reflection
We may feel in your work, lead you.
They lived for us as the fruits of existence

In everything on your earthly journey
That you created in strength and love.

You gaze from spirit heights
Into your friends' hearts;
The fruits of your works of love
Meet your soul's gaze;
They shine through the pain,
In the bright light
That you created for their souls.

Unfailing trust truly known
Was the first spirit-being
That ensouled all your doing.
Whoever experienced this in you
Felt their confidence in their own work
Grow boundless, so that they
Might become one with your work.

The sense of truth that steadfastly
Worked from your clear soul:
Was the second being,
To whom everyone might always draw near
Aspiring to feel related
On the human paths of life.

The third spirit that lived through you
You felt in the warm strength in your soul
That united you to your life work;
It steeled your noble force of love
With unwavering responsibility,
Cloaking the severest deeds of duty
In pure gentleness of heart.

Thus you stood among us,
Fully embodying in your being

The meaning of the work we live;
The place in earthly life
That you gave life to with your strength,
As you enlivened it,
No one else will ever be able to do.

To friends that place in earthly life
Must seem empty;
Yet it will shine brightly
With the spirit flame
That you kindled there with your being.
Powerfully reflected, it will sparkle
In the mirror of your friends' souls.

Lovingly revealed to us
By your earthly sheath,
We hear the eternal human spirit
From those ether heights
With which it now unites,
Proclaiming words of comfort
To the soul-ears of friends, filled with deep sorrow:

"With your earthly work
 I will unite the forces
Available to souls in spirit lands.
Thus, the bond that joined me
To you in temporal being,
The power of the seal of eternity
Will reveal in light and truth."[170]

*

The painter HERMANN LINDE, Sophie Stinde's successor on the board of directors of the Johannesbau-Verein, died in Arlesheim on June 26, 1923, six months after fire destroyed the building in Dornach. In a certain respect, Linde was a victim of that destruction: "It is profoundly true," said Rudolf Steiner, that the fire broke Linde's heart.[171]

Linde, a highly gifted and successful artist, had heard Rudolf Steiner's first lectures in Munich, hosted by Sophie Stinde and Pauline von Kalckreuth, and soon became a member of the German section of the Theosophical Society under Rudolf Steiner. He joined "with sincere enthusiasm, as one of the first of our spiritual community."[172] "Out of deepest self-knowledge, he strove to find the possibility of uniting his own path with that of this spiritual stream."[173] Linde, so said Rudolf Steiner, was a "noble, gentle, and inwardly serious soul."[174] He took this step only after careful consideration and an inner struggle for truth:

> Herman Linde was a gentle soul with a strong, legitimately critical spirit. He tested whatever he encountered; indeed, he had to do so because other preexisting impressions were deeply entrenched in his soul. He struggled inwardly with two streams: on the one hand, everything that filled his soul with warmth but often also with bitter doubt, and on the other, everything that came to him from anthroposo phy, which is so different from anything else one encounters at present.[175]

At his co-worker's cremation in Basel, Rudolf Steiner said more:

> Although Hermann Linde faced doubts and other soul obstacles along the way in his serious approach to spiritual research, he was naturally spiritually inclined and possessed a warm, inward strength of heart that led him powerfully toward his own spirit-word, toward discovering spiritual cognition, which bound him to us in intimate friendship.[176]

12: Hermann Linde (1863-1923)

In inner stillness, solemnity, and dignity, he struggled to overcome all doubts and constraints in the way of the recognition that grants individuals the certainty that what we do and experience on earth has its origins in divine heights of existence. Hermann Linde knew the value of the holy heights of divine existence and saw through the mysteries veiling them, so he also knew how little of what we bring into this existence at birth from heavenly heights actually enters our human consciousness in earthly existence.

While it is true that we are all born out of God into earthly life, our fragile human consciousness does not remain imbued with divine strength during that life. Only in death, experienced through earthly consciousness, can divine strength rediscover the mighty soul power that feels united with the impulse of Christ. Only then is the divine in the human breast reborn, resurrected in union with the Christ.

That was what Hermann Linde felt. Just as he knew that he came from divine existence into earthly existence, he also knew that Christ the Awakener is at work in death and that the human heart and soul can then unite with the Christ.[177]

In Munich, Hermann Linde not only joined the German section of the Theosophical Society under Rudolf Steiner—and took part in the Whitsun Conference of 1907—but also created "wonderfully complete" stage settings for individual scenes in the Mystery Dramas of 1910 to 1913. Linde created these stage settings out of "real experience" of the mystery content; he was *"one of our most effective, devoted, and self-sacrificing workers in Munich. They were his work along with the work of others."*[178] Linde belonged to the inner, meditative study community of what was then the Theosophical Society and to Rudolf Steiner's esoteric school, "but he was also among those who dedicated themselves, with open hearts and boundless readiness to sacrifice, to each new task this spiritual movement asked of them."[179]

In 1910, together with Sophie Stinde and two other friends, Hermann Linde founded the "Theosophical Artistic Fund" in order to finance the Mystery Dramas. A short time later, due to his unquestionable capacity for work and sacrifice and his "conciliatory, loving spirit and ability to balance opposites" (*"which is most needed"*), he was invited to collaborate on the Johannesbau:

> And so Hermann Linde joined the little community that functioned as a committee guiding first our hopes and intentions in Munich and later the reality here in Dornach: constructing a building for the anthroposophical cause.[180]

Rudolf Steiner named Hermann Linde "archdeacon for painting" of the Rosicrucian "Foundation for Theosophical Style and Art" in 1911 and asked him to come to the Johannesbau in Dornach three years later, where Linde participated in the groundbreaking and the laying of the foundation stone. *"And then, when the call came to build the Goetheanum on the hill in Dornach, our building that has also perished, he was again one of the first to offer advice and help and to sacrifice all he had— his art and his very existence—for the sake of the building."*[181]

At Rudolf Steiner's request, Hermann Linde organized the painting of the large dome and worked on it intensively himself, "sacrificing everything he had to offer by way of art for this work, with which he identified totally."[182] In his cremation address and his commemorative talk on the evening of June 29, 1923, Rudolf Steiner recalled his meetings with Hermann Linde in the Johannesbau, under the large dome and in Linde's studio:

> I think back on the hours when I met with Hermann Linde, working alongside our dear friend, his wife, up there under

the dome that no longer exists. There we discussed many different issues related to the building's construction and his role in it. His boundless capacity for sacrifice and willingness to dedicate his artistic ability to what we hoped to achieve was always evident, as were his conciliatory spirit and ability to balance opposites. He was always more ready with advice than with criticism.[183]

These many hours pass before my mind's eye.... He sacrificed his best to that work, and then he (and all of us) had to experience its destruction with profound sorrow.[184]

Herman Linde' work on the Johannesbau was both artistic *and* social. He worked to establish an association of artists: "Out of the infinite goodness of his heart, he attempted to shape their collaborative efforts."[185] He reported regularly on the progress of the artistic work in meetings of the construction committee: "Let us recall things like this, which are intimately related to the history of our movement."[186] He campaigned vigorously on behalf of the threefolding movement (to which he sacrificed his entire private fortune) and initiated the Friedwart School of Continuing Education at the Goetheanum, to which he (like Rudolf Steiner) "devoted particular care and attention."[187] "*We knew it: Of those who worked among us, he was one of the best.*"[188]

*

Rudolf Steiner's connection to Hermann Linde was deep: "Anyone who worked and lived with Hermann Linde and loved and valued human loyalty and human devotion could not fail to esteem and admire this quiet, gentle, yet energetic soul or to sense that he was a most precious friend on our spiritual path."[189] In the cremation address he gave in Basel, Steiner pointed out that in this incarnation, Linde had reached his limits with regard to art and his own identification with it. Rudolf Steiner was extraordinarily satisfied with Linde's work on behalf

13: Goetheanum, May 1921

of anthroposophy even though his overall constitution presented difficulties:

> We who accompanied him were always aware of a strong soul with great intentions occupying a weak body. It was this weak body that took Hermann Linde away from us so early, much too early. His closer associates recognized that all of the obstacles in Hermann Linde's life, even including the doubts that emerged in him and sometimes did not allow his intentions to come to full expression in his work, stemmed from his weak body. Those close to him knew that his soul was large and that he himself often experienced his bodily weakness as an inner tragedy.
>
> For that very reason, however, he found his place in a community of spirit capable of seeing beyond the merely physical, earthly, and sensory aspects of human nature and of looking up to the super-earthly capability that is the greatest goal of the spiritually striving soul. Hermann Linde's close friends often thought, even though you feel unable to realize all your intentions in earthly existence, you may console yourself with the knowledge that your super-earthly will is gaining strength in spirit regions and that you can in fact give the earth everything you would like to give. To ourselves, however, we had to say, we cannot demand as much of Hermann Linde as he does of himself. He was one of the best, and we knew the value of what he accomplished on our behalf.[190]

*

The burning of the Goetheanum—"the Goetheanum so precious to us all, *which has also perished*"—was a severe blow to the anthroposophical movement, and it struck Hermann Linde in his inmost being, in his heart, the organ of destiny and conscience in human existence.[191] In the years after the

end of World War I, Linde had been co-responsible for carry-
ing the heavy burden of completing the Goetheanum and gave
the project everything he had. At the end of 1922, however,
he witnessed the monstrous destruction of this building and
the squandering of its substance of anthroposophy, love, and
sacrifice:

> The impression we experienced on New Year's Eve, the
> death of much of what was of such value to our cause,
> burned deeply in Hermann Linde's soul. The short span of
> time he was still allowed to spend on earth after the burn-
> ing of the Goetheanum was completely dominated by this
> impression.[192]

> This last period of his early existence was a time of suffer-
> ing. In his inmost heart, he had also been deeply affected
> by all the attacks by various opponents of the anthropo-
> sophical movement.[193]

> If pain deepens the life in the spiritual world that follows
> our time on earth, Hermann Linde took a great deal of
> noble pain into the form of existence he has now entered.[194]

The former Johannesbau, the first Goetheanum, "the
building of the anthroposophical cause" upon which much
of the future of "spiritual world culture" depended, was
destroyed by anthroposophy's opponents. The burning of the
Goetheanum, the aggressive attacks on Rudolf Steiner, and
finally the demolition of the remains of the building turned
Linde's life toward death. Linde had been committed to both
the exoteric and esoteric aspects of the building, which was to
be a free school of spiritual science *per signum Michaeli,* a
true Rosicrucian school in the age of Michael. Rudolf Steiner's
cremation address for Hermann Linde pointed to aspects of
spiritual Rosicrucianism, and in his memorial address for

14: The ruins of the first Goetheanum, January 1, 1923

Linde that same evening, Steiner again turned to members of the Anthroposophical Society, saying:

> Today let us recall how beautifully Herman Linde's own heart manifested the conviction that what human beings are and do here on earth stems from the divine: *Ex Deo nascimur*. Let us recall the extent to which forces discovered in his own heart enabled him to acknowledge that the strength of Christ must come alive in human earthly consciousness, so that what begins to die in us at birth wins the hope of new life through experiencing the strength of Christ: *In Christo morimur*. Let us share with Hermann Linde another conviction, calling it to life in our thoughts. When consciousness of our divine-spiritual origin unites with consciousness of union with the Christ-Impulse, we may also live in the conviction that human existence is awakened in spirit, thus becoming conscious of God and Christ-imbued: *Per Spiritum sanctum revivicimus*.
>
> In all times to come, may these thoughts strengthen our ability to direct faithful thoughts upward toward the soul of Hermann Linde, who will continue to work in spiritual existence as a continuation of his earthly existence.[195]

Rudolf Steiner had ended the cremation address in Basel with these words:

> With you today in this solemn hour, beloved soul, we look up into spiritual regions, knowing that those who retain consciousness of their divine origin in earthly existence and who imbue their earthly consciousness with the strength of Christ will be reawakened, resurrected in bright, clear heights of spirit. We accompany you there, soul of our dear friend, with longing glances from deep within our hearts. May you be followed by the best of our thoughts of you. We know that in future you will be in spirit heights. It will

be up to us to seek repeatedly in our hearts' deepest feelings for thoughts to send to you. It will be up to us to unite with your aspiring thoughts in bright spirit heights and to remain with you for all times and through all the cosmic expanses you must traverse. May your thoughts be accompanied by thoughts of ours that derive from the earthly work in which you freely chose to unite with us in spirit during this earthly life.

And you, dear community of mourners, may your thoughts always follow him, linked in spirit, through his future earth-friendly stages of existence in light-filled preparation for a new earthly existence. May it happen thus. Dear Hermann Linde, may our thoughts follow you and stay with you; may we attempt to remain with you even when our souls must seek you in clear spirit heights.

The soft wing-beats of your soul,
Dear friend, bore you on spirit tracks;
Your destiny's solemn guiding hand
Made you prescient of the Spirit-Word.

Many doubts met you on your path, and yet
Your heart's own strength found the way
Through life's light and the shadows of existence
To your thoughts' goal in spirit lands.

And so, true soul friend, behold
In full spirit reality
What weaves before you, shining, full of meaning,
As the future after earthly time.

And, while still in the evening of your life,
Deep in your soul's interior, you saw our greatest pain
Shine terifyingly from the flames:
It broke your heart for earthly being.

Your wife's solemn, heart-felt love

Will follow your spirit life;
Your daughter's true thoughts
Will protect your noble striving

.

And we, united with you in spirit in our earthly life,
We who now usher you into your new life,
We would remain one with you in spirit
In future times and cosmic spaces.[196]

*

The death of the English sculptor EDITH MARYON in the
night of May 1-2, 1924, in Dornach, was announced by Rudolf
Steiner at a class lesson on the evening of May 2:

> For today, it should simply be said that the First Class has
> also lost a truly devoted pupil, for in inner diligence and
> true inwardness, Miss Maryon was foremost among those
> who took up what this class had to offer. In spite of her seri-
> ous illness, she not only took part in esoteric developments
> here but also allowed the exercises given here to work on
> her, living with them in an exceptionally intimate way.
>
> In her case, this is all because she was already an esoteri-
> cist when she came to us. As you know, she had belonged
> to an esoteric school with a totally different path before
> discovering the Anthroposophical Society and quickly
> making a complete transition to anthroposophy. For her,
> the esoteric element was the essential thing. She lived with
> it especially intensively in the years she spent with us on
> the physical plane and will continue to do so now that she
> has left the physical plane—but certainly not anthroposo-
> phy—behind her.[197]

On the following evening (Saturday, May 3), Rudolf Steiner
spoke about Edith Maryon in a lecture to members. Three days

Miss Jeanette Franklin
32 Hyde Park Gardens
W. 2
London
Sende tief schmerzliche Nachricht
Edith Maryon heute gestorben
Rudolf Steiner

15: Text of Rudolf Steiner's telegram to Jeanette Franklin,
May 2, 1924

later, he gave the cremation address in Basel at the conclusion of The Christian Community's ritual for the dead, which was conducted by Friedrich Doldinger.

*

Like his observations at the beginning of the class lesson, Rudolf Steiner's memorial words to members of the Anthroposophical Society emphasized that Edith Maryon came to the anthroposophical movement not only as an artist but also as a trained esotericist:

> The most essential feature of her soul was not any particular branch of human activity, not even art. The most important of her soul tendencies or soul intentions was the striving for spirituality.[198]

Edith Maryon, so said Rudolf Steiner, was distinguished by an esoteric deepening that "she sought continuously within the Anthroposophical Society, for herself and for her soul's striving."[199] Against this background, announcing her death at the beginning of an esoteric class lesson was quite justifiable: *"in inner diligence and true inwardness, Miss Maryon was foremost among those who took up what this class had to offer."*

On the other hand, according to Rudolf Steiner, spiritual deepening as Edith Maryon's central "soul intention" was linked to her absolute intention to contribute to anthroposophical work and to the building in Dornach. Maryon was "animated by a vast and comprehensive intention *to contribute to our work.*"[200] The memorial address given by Rudolf Steiner in the *Schreinerei* as well as extensive passages in the cremation address in Basel dealt with the special quality of Edith Maryon's contribution to "our work."

In November 1915, Rudolf Steiner had described Sophie Stinde's work on behalf of the Anthroposophical Society as "exemplary"; now, nearly nine years later, Steiner once again

lost a central co-worker at the Goetheanum with whom he had
worked with closely, both in building up the Dornach center and
on its central Christ statue. Once again, the times and circumstances were very difficult.[201] On the evening of May 3, 1924,
Rudolf Steiner said of Edith Maryon's artistic collaboration:

> Anthroposophy today, my dear friends, is not only sorely
> contested in the world but also difficult to achieve even
> when taken seriously. Actually, if anthroposophy and the
> anthroposophical movement are taken seriously, the only
> option for individuals is to sacrifice whatever work they
> are capable of contributing on the altar of the Society's
> activity. That is what Miss Maryon did. All of her artistry
> was offered up on the sacrificial altar of the anthropo-
> sophical cause. Through the appropriate schooling, she
> had mastered a type of sculpture accessible to art aficiona-
> dos among the general public, and so forth. Because Miss
> Maryon would have understood, perhaps I may be permit-
> ted to say that all that is actually useless in the anthro-
> posophical movement. Anyone who thinks otherwise is
> on the wrong track. In a certain respect, it is impossible
> to bring anything into the anthroposophical movement.
> Instead, you must first abandon what you once had in
> order to become an active contributor. Anyone who does
> not believe this has not yet fully realized that the anthro-
> posophical movement, if it is to reach its goal, must be a
> totally new creation, drawn from the most primal sources
> of humanity's evolution.[202]

It is quite natural, my dear friends, that from the very
beginning, whatever someone brings in from outside—art
or anything else based on outer education—cannot actually meet with my approval. I beg you to understand this
in the deepest possible sense. Anything brought in from
outside can never meet with my approval. Nonetheless, if

16: Edith Maryon (1872-1924)

the whole is to thrive, individuals need to be able to bring their abilities; sculptors and painters and so on need to be able to contribute their skills. I'm sure you can understand that, because otherwise I would have had to build the entire Goetheanum by myself. Clearly, the Goetheanum needs co-workers who both bring and sacrifice the best of their abilities, because—to put it superficially—I can never actually consent to what they bring from outside.

Of course what I myself was able to accomplish in sculpture was completely different from what Miss Maryon could contribute, so how were we supposed to proceed? The work had to be done the way I had to have it, that is, according to the intentions underlying the Goetheanum, which I was obliged to represent. At this point, a whole new type of interest comes into play, namely, interest in the work itself. To the exclusion of anything else, the people who are part of this work must take an interest in making the work happen. Whether or not we agree with each other, the work must go on; the work must be possible. What I am describing here is necessary for work on the Goetheanum.[203]

Edith Maryon, said Rudolf Steiner, had a profound understanding of what the development of the Goetheanum required, that is, for the prerequisites and demands of Rudolf Steiner's activity on behalf of the spiritual world. Although Miss Maryon had an outstanding artistic education and was extremely competent, she was ready and willing to completely subordinate her work (and the style of her work) to the *"intentions of the Goetheanum."* This process of transformation was one that few could accept, yet it was a prerequisite for work in anthroposophy. In his memorial address and cremation speech, Rudolf Steiner described personal qualities that made Edith Maryon's work on the Goetheanum and in the General Anthroposophical Society so essential, productive, and future-oriented—chief among them her absolute reliability. "There was no chance that anything I intended Miss Maryon to carry out would not happen, that it would not be taken completely seriously or that she would fail to follow my instructions through to the end. This is one quality we need in our anthroposophical work: The fact that I give instructions should be enough to ensure that they are carried out."[204] Steiner also valued Edith Maryon's "practical interest," her "practical sensibilities," her "energetic calmness," and the "calm, quiet way" she worked. From several different perspectives, he described what made the inner quality of Edith Maryon's work "irreplaceable." In the center of her being and activity, however, stood her exemplary relationship to the prerequisites of anthroposophy (and thus also to Rudolf Steiner himself) in developing the school at Dornach into a mystery center for the future. Edith Maryon understood as few others did "what it actually means to lead as I must do it, to work within the anthroposophical movement."[205] On May 3, 1924, Rudolf Steiner spoke of the responsibility this leadership entailed:

> It means that I myself must be in a position to carry whatever happens in connection with me into the spiritual world. I am not responsible simply for what happens here on the physical plane; my responsibility extends into spiritual worlds. If you want to contribute in the right way to what the anthroposophical movement has become since the Christmas Conference, you must come to grips with what it means to take responsibility for the anthroposophical movement and represent it to the spiritual world.[206]

In this connection, Steiner pointed out that many individuals who worked in the Goetheanum and the Anthroposophical Society had "personal aspirations." He characterized this situation and its grave consequences, along with Edith Maryon's totally different behavior:

Suppose those contributing to the anthroposophical movement insert personal ambitions, intentions, and qualities into their work. Most people fail to recognize these personal ambitions and tendencies as such; they deceive themselves, believing they act impersonally. But then these personal emanations must also be presented to the spiritual world, and the backlash on the one who presents them is horrible.

These are the inner difficulties, my dear friends, that arise for a movement such as the anthroposophical movement within the Anthroposophical Society. I need to make you aware of them. It is true and unfortunate that we have terrible opponents, but we must somehow deal with them in the right way. But with regard to the inner aspect of representing anthroposophy, it is much more terrible when work performed in the context of the movement is burdened with personal, individual interests but must nonetheless be carried up into the spiritual world. Little thought is actually given to this fact.

I must mention this as I attempt to characterize Edith Maryon's unique accomplishment. In this regard, the Anthroposophical Society owes great thanks to this departed soul for her ever-growing understanding of how to work in the right way.[207]

As Rudolf Steiner said toward the end of his memorial address in the Dornach *Schreinerei*, Edith Maryon inscribed her activity in the "golden book" of anthroposophy. He asked the members to turn their thoughts toward Maryon's individuality because her own powerfully active thoughts would accompany "the further course of the anthroposophical movement": *"The way she inserted herself into these thoughts will make them powerful. Similarly, connecting with her thoughts will be powerful in its own right."*[208]

*

In the cremation address, Rudolf Steiner gave an extensive description of the course of Edith Maryon's life and her path to Dornach, again via Sophie Stinde's center in Munich. He concluded by dealing with the "germ" of Edith Maryon's fatal illness in the burning of the Goetheanum—like Hermann Linde, she became its victim—and efforts to cure her, undertaken by Steiner together with Ita Wegman, Edith Maryon's "faithful friend and physician."[209]

In a mysterious sentence introducing his commemorative words in the Dornach *Schreinerei*, Rudolf Steiner had already hinted at the fateful antecedents and circumstances of these events: *"Admittedly, the strangest links of destiny are connected to the construction of the first and second Goetheanums."*[210] The cremation address in Basel included Rudolf Steiner's first mention of a momentous event in Edith Maryon's "collaboration with me."[211] She had saved Rudolf Steiner from a potentially fatal fall while working on the Christ statue in the upper studio. Steiner spoke emphatically about a "karmic connection," and later in his address he said:

> I spoke out of awareness of the karmic connection, expressed in pointing to the accident in the studio, when I said that Edith Maryon was predestined to enter the anthroposophical movement and that her death was a cruel loss to the Anthroposophical Society and the entire movement.[212]

In conclusion, Rudolf Steiner gave details about the end of Edith Maryon's life, her treatment and care, and her inner situation—"her attitude, entirely carried by the spirit of anthroposophy, toward the spiritual world she was preparing to enter."[213] In the fifteen months of her illness, Rudolf Steiner had accompanied Edith Maryon wholeheartedly, both outwardly and inwardly. Four months before her death, still hoping for her recovery, he entrusted her with the Section for Fine Arts of the newly founded School of Spiritual Science. To the end, Edith Maryon was occupied with its future development: "Even on her sickbed, her tremendous inner enthusiasm for this work was evident as she constantly attempted to direct her thoughts to how this Section should come about and how it should work."[214]

> Edith Maryon's soul now leaves this life for spiritual worlds, fully imbued with the fruits of anthroposophical spirit-hope and spirit-life. To an extent that few can do, her soul was filled with a vital awareness that the best of her being had emerged from the eternal Father-Spirit's cosmic source: *Ex Deo nascimur*. She lived looking up in inner love to the being who gave the earth's evolution its meaning. In her last days, she had Christ's words "Come to me, you who are troubled and oppressed" fastened to the side of her bed. She knew that in death she would unite with the spirit of Christ: *In Christo morimur*. And so she is assured of a beautiful reawakening in the spiritual world: *Per Spiritum sanctum reviviscimus*. Let us unite with her in her reawakening by sending our thoughts to her so she may unite them with her own.[215]

At the end of the cremation speech, Rudolf Steiner turned directly to Edith Maryon and addressed her individuality. Again he spoke a verse, a true image of her earthly being, to accompany her and support her future activity:

> And so we look up into the spheres where you will lead a life that vanquishes death. We would be with you in a union that never dies but persists, imperishable, through all the cycles of eternity that weave and surge through the cosmos.

Whoever looks upon your karmic path,
Poor in joys,
Will see your noble spirit-striving,
Your warmth of soul:
To them your earthly wandering will reveal
The meaning of a human being's acts.

Whoever feels your presence there,
So still and full of love,
Will see your soul's exertions
That never tired:
To such your daily life reveals
The meaning of a human being's heart.

Whoever stood before your death's door
When it was all-too-close
Will see the hard, painful path
You bore so gently:
To such your sickbed shows
The meaning of a human being's suffering.

Whoever feels your beautiful spiritual work,
So earnestly conducted,
Will behold your life surrendered
To its spiritual end:
To such your soul's struggles now reveal
A human being's power of sacrifice.

Whoever beholds, in the spirit-spheres
Filled with grace,
The future weaving of your soul's life,
Radiant with light:
To such your eternal being
Reveals a human being's spirit-strength.

Whoever sees from the solar heights
So warm with love
Your gaze raying down to us,
Bringing help:
To such your spirit actions now reveal
A human being's power to bless.

Then Rudolf Steiner closed and completed the cremation address with these words:

So go now, you soul so truly devoted to our cause! Let us look up to you. We know you are looking down on us; we know that we remain united with you through all cycles of eternity. As long as we are here, we will continue to live with you as you live the life that conquers death, and when we are no longer here, we shall continue living with you: united, united, united.[216]

*

Wer da blickt
~~Ich blicke~~ auf deinen Karmaweg
   Den freudearmen,
Der
~~Ich~~ schaut dein edles Geistesstreben
   Das seelen – warme:
~~Und~~ Ihm
  ~~mir~~ erscheint eines Menschenwesens Wirkenssinn
   Aus deinem Erdenwandel –

Wer da,
~~Ich~~ fühlt dein so stilles Sein
   Das liebevolle
Der
~~Ich~~ schaut deiner Seele Mühen
   Das nie ermüdende
~~Und~~ Ihm
  ~~mir~~ erscheint eines Menschenwesens Herzenssinn
   Aus deinem Tagesleben. –

Wer da stand
~~Ich stand~~' vor deinem Todestore
   Dem allzunahen,
Der
~~Ich~~ schaut den harten Schmerzensweg
   den sanft ertragenen:
~~Und~~ Ihm
  ~~mir~~ erscheint eines Menschenwesens Duldersinn
   Von deinem Krankenlager.

Wer empfindet
~~Ich bin beglückt von~~ deinem ~~seligen~~ Geisteswert
Der
  ~~Den~~ ernst geführtest,
~~Ich~~ schaut dein Leben hingegeben
   Dem Geistes – Teile:
  Ihm
  ~~mir~~ erscheint eines Menschenwesens Opferkraft
   Aus deinem Seelenringen.

17: Rudolf Steiner – Text of the verse for Edith Maryon (1924)

Wer da\
~~Ich~~ schaut in *der* Geistes – Sphären\
    Den\
    ~~Ihr~~ segensvollen\
Dein Seelenleben künftig weben\
    Das Licht – erstrahlende\
Und ~~mir~~ *Ihm* erscheint eines Menschenwesens Geistes *Kraft*\
    Aus deinem Ewig – Sein.

Wer da\
~~Ich~~ schauet aus *der* Sonnenhöhen\
    Der\
    ~~Aus~~ liebenswarmen\
Deinen Blick zu uns herniederstrahlen\
    Den hilfe – spendenden\
~~Und mir~~ *Ihm* Erscheint eines Menschenwesens Segenskraft\
    Aus deinem ~~deines~~ ~~Sternenwesens~~\
    Geisteswirken, —

II

"In Christo Morimur"

The Path of the Soul after Death[217]

Let me not neglect to gradually
give our friends some idea of these circumstances,
which are so difficult to depict.

— RUDOLF STEINER[218]

We can accept and understand these issues
if we repeatedly think them through anew.
Their inherent energy makes them comprehensible
to our souls.[219]

T HE PROCESS OF DYING is intrinsic to human life. Far from
being an abrupt and foreign intrusion into an individual's
vital life processes, it is inherent in them, shaping the conditions that make our earthly existence possible. Conscious or
near-conscious experience imposes limits on our purely vital
processes—experience takes shape at a cost to life, consciousness at a cost to being. In a certain sense, experience and
consciousness are postulated on the limitation or even the sacrifice of life and being.[220] In this sense, death process are part and
parcel of human physiology, especially the physiology of the
organs and functions that support and serve our waking day-consciousness on earth—that is, the human sensory-nervous
system.[221] In 1917 Rudolf Steiner said:

> Inasmuch as we make mental images, death is active in us
> all the time. That is, death is always present and active in a
> fragmentary way, and our ultimate death simply sums up
> all the breakdown activities constantly at work in us. Of
> course much of this breakdown is counteracted, although
> in the end it does result in spontaneous death. We must
> understand death as an active force in the organism just as
> we understand life forces.[222]

Death, says Steiner, is an "ongoing process."[223] Death forces
are a permanent feature of the human body, or more specifically of our past-oriented sensory-nervous system (which works

out of old forces) and of the intellectual and spiritual development it indirectly facilitates: *The process that takes place one time only at a person's physical death, when it affects the entire human organism, accompanies human existence throughout life as a potential or even as the constantly emerging beginning of the death process.*"[224]

During a lifetime, however, death's processes and tendencies are always counteracted by active vital forces, overcome and actively transformed by the forces of the metabolic-limb system, which are oriented toward the present and the future.[225] A person's actual death sets in only when any such counteracting forces are exhausted or incisively altered.[226] Only then is the lifelong "fragmentary" dying of the sensory-nervous system "summed up," as Steiner put it, resulting in an intensification of the ever-present tendency toward suppression or even physiological destruction of life. The poles of human earthly existence— birth and death—represent both the maximal development and the limits of the functional processes of building up and breaking down, anabolism and catabolism, shaping the body and overcoming the body:

> For mathematicians, we might say that actual birth is an integral of all the "birth differentials" present throughout life. Similarly, "death differentials" are also present, and actual death is only their integral. Inwardly, we are constantly dying, but this dying is counteracted in the moment it occurs. That is the material basis of our conceptual activity. The moment of actual death is simply an infinite intensification of an ongoing activity in us, just as actual birth is an infinite intensification of the ongoing process of growth. Here we see the soul-spiritual and bodily-material processes in one.[227]

In this sense, a human being's death is part of the individual's earthly existence. Interwoven with life processes, it is a fundamental condition of the "I"'s ongoing gesture of incarnation as it develops and gains experience through the biographical process.

*

Eventually, processes of death and dying overwhelm the organism's vital being and diseases develop, paving the way for death.[228] These disease processes build up to the ultimate "integral of dying," when the individual's spiritual/soul/physical makeup changes in an instant. In describing the loosening of the etheric body of formative forces (along with the astral and I-organization) from the physical body, Rudolf Steiner says that in the moment of death, the configuration of spiritual forces that once supported, pervaded, and vitalized the processes of the physical body loses its functional connection with the organism and abandons the physical structure to set out on its path toward the future in the spiritual world. "The phenomenon of death sets in like this: In the moment of death, the connection of the etheric and astral bodies to the physical bodies dissolves—specifically, in the heart. The heart is illuminated, so to speak, and then the etheric body, astral body, and "I" rise up above the head."[229]

Rudolf Steiner calls this the *"moment of having died."*[230] He describes this separation from physical existence and thus from earthly connections as having incisive, lasting importance for the human individuality's entire further path:

> That the physical body remains behind on earth is of major, even crucial, significance when we pass through the portal of death. We go into the spiritual world; we leave our physical body behind on earth. The so-called deceased experience this as the "departure" of their body. It is a great and powerful experience that cannot be compared to any event in earthly existence.[231]

The spiritual grandeur and dignity of the event of death is intimately connected to the physical body's "departure," which the individuality experiences so deeply while leaving the earth.[232] Passing through the moment of death makes concrete I-consciousness in the spiritual world possible: *"If we were unable to have this experience when passing through the portal of death, if we did not knowingly experience the departure of our physical body, we would never be able to develop I-consciousness after death."*[233] That I-consciousness or self-awareness—greatly enhanced, by earthly standards—belongs to the onward-leading character of the individuality's path after death; it could not be stimulated and developed without experiencing the physical body "falling away from the human being as a whole."[234] As Rudolf Steiner emphasized in various lectures, the ways in which I-consciousness develops at the beginnings of postnatal and posthumous life are, in a sense, polar opposites; they manifest in diametrically opposed relationships to our physical, bodily nature. Earthly development of I-consciousness is accomplished through adaptation of the spirit-soul to the physical and etheric bodily nature that increasingly reflects it.[235] By contrast, development of I-consciousness or self-awareness after death develops as a result of *overcoming* that same physical-etheric nature: "It is true that the human soul entering existence through birth (or even as early as conception) gradually adapts to using the physical apparatus and thus acquires I-consciousness in the body. It is equally true that after death, I-consciousness is acquired from the opposite side, by experiencing the physical body falling away from the human being as a whole."[236] As Rudolf Steiner emphasized in Berlin on December 7, 1921, the event of death, which inherently entails releasing the human individuality from its physical-etheric context, makes it possible to experience the physical body as a whole for the first time. Distance makes this perception possible:

> When we attempt to perceive and understand something, we can do so only if our intended object is outside of us.

You do not see what is inside your eye; you see only what is *outside* of it. The same is true of spiritual soul vision. In order to see the body, the spirit and soul must be outside the body. This happens at the moment of death, when the etheric and physical bodies fall away. Only in dying, in the moment of death, do we have our entire physical body in front of us as an object. For the entire time between death and a new birth, this impression persists as the endpoint of our view when we look back after death. We see this moment of dying because we would not recognize our "I" as such—that is, we would be without an "I"—if the object of cognition at the moment of death were not what we bring to consciousness here in the physical world, namely, our entire physical body. Beholding the entire physical body, the gift of I-consciousness, in the moment of death makes a tremendous impression. That impression endures and forms the content of I-consciousness between death and rebirth, when everything becomes temporal and the spatial aspect, in a certain respect, no longer exists. When we look back from any point after death, we see the moment of death as an important point, the endpoint of our view. (Actually, the line of sight continues, but the lines cross in the moment of the most recent death.) After death, this "temporal member," if I may put it like that, provides I-consciousness, just as the spatial-physical organism does between birth and death.[237]

As early as September 6, 1915, in a lecture in Dornach on the immediate posthumous developments with regard to the physical body's significance for consciousness, Rudolf Steiner put it similarly:

Now [in the time after death] we look at our physical body. It lives in our consciousness; it becomes one of the contents of our consciousness. By remembering our physical body, so to speak, we know ourselves to be an "I" for the entire time between death and a new birth. Knowing we once had this physical body takes the place of actually having it. A state of consciousness, a conscious phenomenon, replaces the body itself. The overall sense of the physical body that we have from birth to death is replaced after death by *consciousness* of our physical body.[238]

*

Rudolf Steiner described the "moment of having died" as the "consummate event."[239] During the individuality's time away from earth, this moment is constantly in view.[240] It is filled with beauty, grandeur, and bright, sun-like, Christ-related warmth.[241] It is essential not only to developing but also to dynamically maintaining self-awareness specifically adapted to the spiritual world. In this connection, Rudolf Steiner said in Kassel on February 18, 1916:

> Throughout human life between death and a new birth, it is possible to look back on the moment of death, and therefore that moment provides our consciousness after death. We know that we have laid aside our physical body. Knowing this and having it constantly before us gives us our self-awareness after death, just as we derive self-awareness here in the physical world from actually having a physical body.
>
> When we are outside of the physical body with our astral body and "I," between falling asleep and waking up again, we have no consciousness of the physical world. When awakening, we must re-occupy these bodies so that I-consciousness can blossom again. After death, whenever we look back on the moment of dying, whenever that whole event—which is so grand and beautiful from the perspective of the other side—stands before our soul, consciousness is rekindled. *Consciousness after death depends entirely on repeated viewing of this moment.*[242]

In Leipzig four days later, Rudolf Steiner explained further:

> Once beyond the portal of death, any moments when we
> are not beholding the moment of death are to posthumous
> I-consciousness as sleep is to physical I-consciousness
> here. When asleep, we know nothing of our physical
> I-consciousness. Similarly, after death, we are unaware of
> ourselves whenever we do not have that moment of dying
> in view.[243]

When we look back over our life in the body, the earthly experience of birth eludes our consciousness, but its opposite, the
experience of death, persists as we enter and dwell in the spiritual world. It becomes the starting point of the ongoing development of consciousness: "In the spiritual worlds, we possess
this I-consciousness as a result of inwardly creating ourselves on
an ongoing basis. We never appeal to a static existence but are
constantly creating ourselves. This process of self-creation is like
reaching back to ourselves through time to the moment when
death occurred."[244] In other accounts, Rudolf Steiner said:

> When we look back in time after death, it is as if we ulti-
> mately come to death itself, and arriving at the moment
> of death in this temporal view is what provides lasting
> I-consciousness after death. So this I-consciousness is also
> a reflection; it is reflected back to us from the fact of our
> death.[245]

> Perceiving our "I" between death and a new birth is always
> like saying to ourselves, you really died, therefore you are
> I, you are an "I"! It is of utmost importance to look back
> on the spirit's victory over the body, on the moment of
> death, which is the most beautiful moment that can be
> experienced in the spiritual world. In looking back, we
> become aware of our Self in the spiritual world.[246]

From the earthly perspective, the moment of dying and the beginning of the physical body's irreversible decay seem tragic. From the perspective of the spiritual world and to the human individuality entering it, however, these events appear as a shining "victory of spirit" over physical nature, "the process by which the spirit extricates itself from the physical."[247] They mark the actual beginning of life in the spirit and are accompanied by intense experiences: *In the spiritual worlds, I-consciousness is present in feeling the spirit's self-creating life force.*[248]

In considering the first stages of the soul's posthumous life, however, it must be noted that what lies behind the deceased's initial development of consciousness is not unconsciousness but rather a genuine "superabundance of consciousness": "What sets in at death is not a lack of consciousness but quite the opposite. Too much consciousness, a superabundance of consciousness, is present when death has set in. We then live and work entirely in consciousness, and just as bright sunlight blinds our eyes, we are initially blinded by too much consciousness. This consciousness must be subdued before we can orient ourselves in the life we enter after death."[249] Developing new, posthumous I-consciousness after death actually requires "suppressing" or "toning down" consciousness: "We wake up when we succeed in restricting our capacity for orientation to what we can bear. The overabundance of consciousness that sets in after death must be suppressed to a degree that we can tolerate."[250] "In a certain sense, we are unconscious after death because consciousness is too strong, too forceful. After death we live entirely in consciousness, and during the first few days we must come to grips with this state of excessive consciousness and orient ourselves in it. When we manage to orient ourselves enough to be able to feel 'That was you!' in the plethora of cosmic thoughts, when we begin to distinguish our past earthly life, we come to a moment of awakening in this superabundance of consciousness."[251] According to Rudolf Steiner, however, this waking process is bound up with focusing on the experience of death, the "moment of having died": "We must look back on the moment in our development when we passed through death, *and we must recognize ourselves there.*"[252] In Nuremberg on March 31, 1915, Rudolf Steiner offered further clarification:

> [The deceased] orients herself by looking back on her own earthly life and her character in that life. She must orient herself through self-knowledge, which is the point of attachment for the orienting force and the starting point for subduing the excess of consciousness to a level she can tolerate. This varies depending on what she went through in her last incarnation. What actually happens, therefore, is that the excess of consciousness is suppressed to a level the individual can tolerate.[253]

Self-experience in the death event—in the "moment of having died"—and the subsequent review of one's biography and character (perhaps aided and accompanied by memorials conducted by friends and relatives remaining on earth) open the way for acquiring a new orientation in the "excess of cosmic thoughts" in the suprasensible world after death.

*

When the physical body is released and left behind, it soon unites with the being and future of the earth.[254] According to Rudolf Steiner, constantly returning to this "moment of having died" not only makes consciousness possible but is also a profound spiritual experience of "emptiness." Although the spirit-soul now experiences the cosmos dense with active forces, it simultaneously experiences the emptiness of the abandoned space of its past embodied existence: *In life between death and a new birth, we—along with the suprasensible forces that underlay our physical body here—actually occupy the entire cosmos, except for one place that remains empty. That is the space, bounded by our skin, that we occupy here in the physical world.*"[255] In its onward-leading, consciousness-facilitating aspects, "constantly viewing" the moment of death implies encountering and dealing with this emptiness or "hollowness."[256] In fact, it *is* that emptiness:

> Described in such theoretical terms, this situation sounds somewhat gruesome, but there is nothing gruesome about perceiving it after death; in fact, it fills the soul with profound satisfaction. We learn to spread out into the whole world, as it were, and to look at a space that remains empty. This, then, is our perception: That is your place in the world, a space apart from all the world's expanses, and it is yours alone. Specifically as a result of this emptiness, we perceive that we have meaning and purpose for the entire world. We experience—of course at first with regard to ourselves—the necessity of each individual human existence. As a human being, each one of us has a designated space in the cosmos, and this unbelievably warming inner perception emerges from the observation that within the existence of the entire cosmos, a single note resounds as if in a symphony, and that note is the fact that we exist—and must exist, or the cosmos would not be there. *This perception results from looking back on the event of death. It persists, not the least because it enables I-consciousness or self-awareness between death and a new birth.*[257]

This crucial perception of the justification and necessity of one's individual existence, which supports and substantiates the further life of the spirit-soul on its journey after death, therefore "makes up much of what we call the afterlife."[258] Ultimately, this perception is based on the experience of "emptiness" in the "moment of having died":

> It is the perception of something in the world that must be repeatedly filled by you. You then arrive at the perception that you are in the world for a purpose that only you can

fulfill. You sense your place in the world; you sense that you are one of the building blocks without which the world could not exist. That is what our perceiving this emptiness does. Awareness of belonging to the world comes over us as a result of looking at an empty space.[259]

*

According to Rudolf Steiner, during the first few days after death, the etheric body of formative forces, which has separated from the organism of physical forces along with the spirit-soul organization, still remains partially united with the spirit-soul. Thereafter, however, it also (mostly) separates from the human individuality and is integrated or "tied" into the sphere of the etheric world.[260, 261] Again, intense experiences are associated with this posthumous process. The individualized etheric body had been the temporal vehicle of an earthly life story, the body of memory and recollection.[262] Now, in the process of freeing itself from the constraints of physicality, it unfolds "objectively" before the individuality's consciousness:

> The unique aspect of this tableau immediately after death is that it omits all subjective experiences in our earthly journey. In the course of various experiences in life, we always have feelings of pleasure and pain, elation and sadness; our outer perception is always linked to inner activity. When we look back on this tableau, however, we see no joys and sorrows attached to these images of life. We confront the tableau as objectively as if it were a painting. When we look at a painting that depicts a man who is sad or sorrowful, we can empathize with his sadness but we cannot feel his pain directly. It is the same with the images in the tableau immediately after death. It spreads out in front of us, and in an astonishingly short time, we see all the details of what befell us during life.[263]

This "tableau of memories," the images and "details" of the
life just lived, stand before the human soul with consummately
imaginative presence and simultaneity:

> Everything we experienced in life, even the most minor
> event, is suddenly there as if in a great tableau of our life
> that persists for days.
>
> In this process, we get a strong sense that the earth we
> formerly stood upon has moved on, leaving us behind.
> We are no longer accompanying the earth on its journey
> through space. And meanwhile the tableau of our life
> spreads out in front of us....
>
> In mighty images, it presents our experiences of the
> time just before death, simultaneously with our childhood
> experiences. A panorama of our life, an image containing
> all these events that occurred in succession, is present in a
> tapestry woven out of the ether. Everything we see there
> lives in the ether.
>
> Above all, we experience everything around us as alive.
> Everything is alive and at work. Then we also experience
> it through spiritual sound, spiritual light, and spiritual
> warmth.[264]

This image-filled panorama of experiences is due to the
etheric body's dissolution, release, and expansion.[265] "It is
the individual's first experience after death."[266] In its essence,
says Rudolf Steiner, the panorama is a "tableau of thoughts";
it includes *everything we experienced through thinking and
creating mental images.*[267]

It is actively created and shaped by the spirit-soul's forces of
will and feeling.[268] It consists, however, of the thought-forces
of earthly existence, the thought-imbued, conscious (or at least
potentially conscious) experiences of the completed biography.[269] It is made up, as Steiner describes, of *"thought-images
of our experiences."*[270]

We behold these thoughts. Instead of bringing them up from depths related to the physical body, we behold them in an overview, as if in a panorama of the life we have just completed.[271]

*

In this process of beholding, the individual, along with the entire image, is freed from the body-shaping and thought-bearing forces of an individual earthly biography and from the modes of experience those forces made possible. This separation takes place as feeling and will unite a specific etheric dimension of the past incarnation with the "objective thought-world of the etheric cosmos.[272] As such, the individual etheric body does not dissolve; it has active consequences for the cosmic ether-world and the beings at work in it:

> What we acquired during life on behalf of our etheric body gradually becomes part of the spiritual world. We must realize, however, that all the thoughts and feelings we develop, no matter how hidden they remain, have significance for the spiritual world. Together with our etheric body, they enter that world and contribute to it after they are torn from their physical context at our passage through the portal of death.[273]

The human etheric body is transformed and subsumed into the etheric cosmos or "world ether substantiality" and the beings that work in it.[274] These beings receive human etheric bodies with gratitude: "The heavens are full of gratitude for everything human beings acquire during life through work and through thinking, feeling, and willing. The heavens appreciate the consequences that appear in our etheric bodies. If we turn our clairvoyant vision toward an etheric body that a human being has laid aside, we are overwhelmed as if by a cloud of gratitude."[275]   Thus the human body of formative forces acquires importance and impact in the cosmos, where it manifests in image form. It persists, always remaining perceptible or spiritually visible to the individual, unlike the temporary "life tableau":[276]

> It unites with the entire universe but remains visible to us in the process. The mysteries of death include not only the panorama of thoughts we had in life, which persist only as long as we are still attached to the etheric body, but also the etheric body's incorporation into the world outside of us, so that after death it belongs to our surroundings instead of to our "I."[277]

To the individual spirit-soul setting out on the path after death, this view of the cosmically transformed and incorporated etheric body is "shattering in its loftiness, a very powerful event indeed."[278] Through this view, the individuality of the deceased experiences being drawn into the supporting sphere of the universe, becomes aware of the reality and consequence of earthly actions (and sensations and intentions) for the existence and development of the world, and develops a "cosmic consciousness."[279] The individuality encounters the "cosmic archetypal image of the human being" and thus the ultimate Christological foundation of conscience.[280] Simultaneously, the specific spirituality of the cosmic-etheric world is experienced; the individuality begins to understand it as a result of the successive transformation and incorporation of the individual etheric body. Rudolf Steiner also described this situation on February 18, 1916, again emphasizing the enduring character of this perception:

> We see it constantly. We are always looking at it; it is part of our outer world. What was once in our etheric body, as part of our inner world, now belongs to the outer world.

18: Notebook entry by Rudolf Steiner (1924)

3.) Through the moments after death comes to light,
how the human being is related to the whole world =
Parts of the human being go to the parts of the world —
Space bearer of cosmic thoughts.

It is important to be able to look at it because the relationship between what we ourselves incorporated into
our etheric body and the entire spiritual outer world is
what makes many aspects of the spiritual outer world
understandable.[281]

In this sense, the cognitive work an individuality accomplished during the most recently completed biography becomes
an organ of perception for the etheric cosmos. The scope and
quality of the "relationship" between individualized thought-
activity and objective world-thought determine the degree of
spiritual immanence; simultaneously, they make it possible for
the individuality to "bear" the full brunt of etheric wisdom and
strength. On our path after death, the cosmic-etheric wisdom we
experience threatens to overwhelm us: "...*and it would continue
to overwhelm us if we were incapable of inserting what we
incorporated into the etheric body during life into that world. If
we are able to do this, the result is a dimming of the tremendous
superabundance of light in the general world-ether such that we
can begin to understand what weaves through it, pervading the
world with soul and spirit.*"[282]

This understanding, together with the associated "etheric
tableau" (which precedes it, is visible to the individuality, and
is absorbed into the cosmos), contributes to strengthening the
I-consciousness and self-perception characteristic of the individual's posthumous path.[283] The ongoing experience of "emptiness" also contributes.[284] In Hamburg on February 2, 1916,
Rudolf Steiner elaborated on these connections in reference to
the essentially thought-like character of the etheric body:

Everything thought-like in character becomes an outer
world. After death, we do not look at our thoughts as we
looked at thoughts developed and then remembered during
life, recalled from subconscious depths. After death, we
look at our thoughts like an etheric painting; we see them

out there in the world. Thoughts become externalized for those who have passed through the portal of death. What is revealed to us here on earth through feeling and will remains connected to our individuality and continues to live in our astral body and our I. In the I, self-awareness is kindled by viewing the moment of death; in the astral body, it is kindled when the thoughts in the "painting" before us break in on it. That is how we experience them in our astral body.[285]

In this sense, the strengthening of individual self-experience at the beginning of the posthumous path has its origin in the human I-organization and astral body. Consciousness is "kindled" in ways specific to each of these two levels of being— in the I through the experience of the physical body, "going away" (or being left behind) and through the resulting emptiness, in the soul-body through the etheric body's expansion and the incorporation of a life's worth of thoughts into the cosmos in a process that is "reflected" in the soul-body.[286]

*

Ultimately, in order to process and overcome the earthly biography on a new level and create the prerequisites for actual cosmic spirit-experience, the astral organization must also separate from the human individuality as the posthumous journey continues. Since the end of the three-day "review" of the past life, the astral body has served as the vehicle of the completed earthly incarnation's outcomes.[287] Rudolf Steiner describes the astral body's dissolution in terms of breaking the soul-habits of earthly modes of experience, a process that takes decades but begins soon after the event of earthly death. Breaking these habits takes place in the sphere of warmth.[288] Renouncing earthly habits must be understood as a process that tears the individual out of previously experienced contexts and is therefore also a step in overcoming the world of feelings and aspirations.[289] According to Rudolf Steiner, the beginning of this process coincides with the obliteration of the etheric life-tableau just a few days after earthly death. Unlike the etheric process, the astral body's dissolution does not take place in the world of active thoughts but in the sphere of "feeling will":

> From now on, the soul's experience is neither feeling nor willing but something in between, which I will call "willing feeling" or "feeling will." This newly emerging soul force is not one we know at all in ordinary life. It is as if our will moves through the world taking us with it; on its wings or in its flow it supports feeling that approaches us from outside, as if on waves of willing. We are otherwise accustomed to being inwardly attached to feeling, but it now approaches from outside as if weaving and surging on waves of will. Since we know we are expanding into the world, we also know that our own being now pervades the willing feeling or feeling will that is now outside in the same way that perceptions of color and sound are outside us in the sensory world. We perceive external feeling the way we once perceived light, but in perceiving it we recognize that we are related to it.
>
> Once the etheric review of life ends, we experience that the world we then perceive is basically the world we left behind at death. After the tableau of memory fades, feeling will or willing feeling develops in the soul, gaining strength, but all of its manifestations are still connected to the earthly life just past.[290]
>
> Between the lines of life, so to speak, certain aspects of our desires, wishes, love for other people, and so forth, still persist. For many years, our spiritual gaze looks back with desire on anything that remained "unresolved"—to use a trivial expression—in our last life. In these years, our world consists primarily in what we once were. We

look back into our most recent earthly existence and behold whatever remained unresolved in that lifetime. In this sphere, none of our desires are satisfied because we have laid aside the bodily organs of their satisfaction. We spend years in this sphere before we manage to extricate our soul from such connections to our most recent earthly life.[291]

During the dissolution of the astral body, the feelings, desires, and striving impulses of the most recent earthly biography are experienced in the form of the individuality's immediate surroundings and outer world. (*"Feelings are our outer world."*[292]) The individuality beholds the world turned inside out, lives in its "reflection" in the I, and must overcome it through renunciation, dehabituation, and transformation.[293] This period after death, though of long duration, is not static. Rather, the individuality passes through the most recent earthly biography with great inner dynamism and in reverse direction: "In fact, time reverses and returns to its starting point."[294] We experience the soul-consequences of our own actions from the perspective of those affected by them: *"[On earth,] we actually only experience half of what happens because of us."*[295] This process of working back through the past lifetime recovers and completes the soul's biography.[296] The recapitulation involves a moral assessment of the individual's completed life story.[297] Furthermore, it involves the development of an unconscious karma-will.[298] Finally, after decades, the recapitulation reaches back to the biography's beginning, leading to release both from the earth-imbued astral organization (as reflected in the I) and from the most recent earthly life:[299]

> Having gone all the way back to birth, we have matured enough to lay aside the aspect of the astral body that is saturated with earthly influences. That aspect falls away from us and a new stage begins. The astral body is what

always tied our experiences to the earth. Throughout the passage through the astral body—not in a dream, but by re-experiencing earthly events in reverse—we were still present in earthly life. We are totally free from the earth only once we have "laid aside" the astral body. (That is not actually what happens, but our language has no word for it.) Then we live in the actual spiritual world.[300]

In his book *Theosophy*, Rudolf Steiner sums up this process of release as follows:

> When its own forces can no longer support the human soul organization, the soul releases the spirit into the higher (spiritual) world. The spirit is freed when the soul relinquishes to dissolution its experiences that are possible only in the body but retains those that can live on in the company of spirit. Although what remains was also experienced in the body, it was imprinted on the spirit as the fruits of experience. The soul links this remnant to the spirit in the purely spiritual world.
>
> To learn about the fate of the soul after death, we must therefore consider its dissolution process. Its job was to direct the spirit toward the physical. In the moment this task is completed, the soul turns to the spirit. [...] Because the spirit becomes very closely related to the soul during life (much more closely than to the body), it remains tied to the soul to the last minute. The spirit relates to the body indirectly, via the soul, but is directly connected to the soul itself. The soul is the spirit's independent existence.[301]

After its release from the earth and the soul, the spirit sets out on its journey with the help of the Christ.[302] This journey in the "actual spiritual world," as a "spirit among spirits," lasts many hundreds of years.[303] It serves as preparation for the following earthly incarnation and its task.[304] It also serves to "preserve the holiness of life."[305]

Until the last months of his life, Rudolf Steiner continued to describe this journey in many other lectures.

Notes

[The page numbers cited in these notes indicate pages in the German volumes from the Gesamtausgabe (GA). See the Literature Cited section beginning on p. 167 for information on the English titles, when available.]

1 Rudolf Steiner, *Unsere Toten*, p. 200.
2 Ibid., p. 199.
3 Ibid., p. 27.
4 Rudolf Steiner: *Die Verbindung zwischen Lebenden und Toten*, p. 17.
5 Rudolf Steiner: *Mein Lebensgang*, p. 59.
6 "Es warten aber / der scheuen Augen viele / Zu schauen das Licht." Friedrich Hölderlin: *Patmos*. In: *Sämtliche Werke*. Stuttgarter Hölderlin-Ausgabe, Vol. 2. Stuttgart 1951, p. 170.
7 Friedrich Rittelmeyer: "Rudolf Steiner als Ereignis in der Geschichte des Christentums." In: *Die Christengemeinschaft*, Vol. 2, Issue 2, April 1925, p. 40.
8 Rudolf Steiner: *Unsere Toten*, p. 200.
9 Rudolf Steiner: *Das Geheimnis des Todes*, p. 334.
10 Rudolf Steiner: *Die Welt des Geistes und ihr Hereinragen in das physische Dasein*, p. 65.
11 Cf. Rudolf Steiner, *Mein Lebensgang*, p. 118f., where Steiner recounts his friendship with the Fehr siblings and his frequent visits to their home. Steiner continues:
    "In this family, an unseen presence hovered in the background. It was the young people's father, who was there but also not there. We heard widely varying accounts about this peculiar person. Initially, the siblings did not mention their father at all, although he must have been in the next room. They only gradually began to make one or the other

comment about him, their words imbued with true awe and
veneration. We sensed that he was a revered and important
figure to them, but we also sensed their trepidation that some
coincidence might bring us face to face with him.

Our conversations with this family were generally
about literature, and in this connection the siblings sometimes fetched books from their father's library. As time went
on, therefore, although I never saw the man in the next room,
I became familiar with much of what he read. In the end,
I could not avoid asking many questions relating to him,
and a mental picture of his remarkable personality gradually emerged from the siblings' reticent yet much-revealing
remarks. I, too, came to love and value this man. In the end, I
revered him as a person compelled by difficult life experiences
to limit his worldly involvement to inner activity and to avoid
all interaction with others.

One day when we visited, we were told the man was
ill, and a short time later we were informed of his death. The
sisters and their brother entrusted me with the funeral eulogy.
I expressed what my heart told me about this person, whom I
had gotten to know only in the way described above. Only the
family, the fiancé of one of the daughters, and my friends were
present at the burial. The siblings told me that my address had
given an accurate picture of their father. Their way of speaking
and their tears confirmed their estimation, and I realized the
man was as close to me in spirit as if I had actually frequented
his company."

12   There is no stenographic record of Rudolf Steiner's address
at Christian Morgenstern's cremation and no record of his
overall organization of this commemorative event.

13   Cf. Peter Selg: *Christian Morgenstern. Sein Weg mit Rudolf
Steiner*. Stuttgart 2008.

14   Of the circumstances leading up to this development, Michael
Debus writes:

The specific occasion that prompted the communication of the funeral service, as the first in a complete series
of renewed religious rituals, was the burial of Marie Hahn on

September 22, 1918, which marked the beginning of Rudolf
Steiner's collaboration with Hugo Schuster. Marie Hahn was
the first wife of Hugo Hahn (d. 1932), the stenographer of
many of Rudolf Steiner's lectures. Rudolf Steiner spoke at
Marie's funeral at Hugo's request, but on the condition that
his address be preceded by a denominational service. The
Hahns, however, had long since dropped any connection to
their church, so Rudolf Steiner turned to the Reverend Hugo
Schuster, who conducted the service according to the Old
Catholic rite. Rudolf Steiner then gave his address, beginning
with the words, "Now that priestly words have guided the
soul we love from the visible to the invisible world...." After
the funeral, according to Hahn's later report, Rudolf Steiner
commented that the Old Catholic ritual was "just too inad-
equate" and something fundamentally new would have to be
created. (Michael Debus: "Der Totenkultus und die anthroposophische Bewegung." In: Michael Debus/Gunhild Kacer:
Das Handeln im Umkreis des Todes. Fragen zur Bestattung.
Stuttgart 1996, p. 15f.).

15   Ibid., p. 16.

16   Rudolf Steiner: *Esoterischer Betrachtungen karmischer Zusammenhänge.* Vol. II, p. 284.

17   Debus, op. cit, p. 16.

18   On the spiritual reality of the "ritual (or sacrament) of ordina-
tion," cf. explanations in Rudolf Steiner's lectures of October
3 and 10, 1921. In: Rudolf Steiner: *Spirituelles Erkennen.
Religiöses Empfinden. Kultisches Handeln. Vorträge und
Kurse über christlich-religiöses Wirken, II.*

19   Rudolf Steiner: *Esoterische Bretrachtungen karmischer
Zusammen-hänge.* Vol. II, p. 284f.

20   Cf. in this context Wolfgang Gädeke: *Anthroposophy und
die Fokrtbildung der Religion.* Flensburg 1990, p. 374f, and
Gunhild Kacer: "Fragen zur Bestattung." In: *Das Handeln
im Umkreis des Todes,* p. 21f.

21   Rudolf Steiner: *Vom Wesen des wirkenden Wortes. Vorträge
und Kurse über christlich-religiöses Wirken IV,* p. 11.

22   Ibid., p. 43f. Emphasis added.

23   Rudolf Gädeke: Friedrich Doldinger, in: Gädeke: *Die Gründer der Christengemeinschaft. Ein Schicksalsnetz.* Dornach 1992, p. 125.

24   Steiner: *Unsere Toten,* p. 276.

25   Steiner: *Das Geheimnis des Todes,* p. 321.

26   Rudolf Steiner: *Okkulte Untersuchungen über das Leben zwischen Tot und neuer Geburt,* p. 330.

27   Ibid., p. 326f.

28   Steiner: *Das Geheimnis des Todes,* p. 346.

29   Steiner: *Unsere Toten,* p. 36.

30   Steiner: *Die Welt des Geistes und ihr Hereinragen in das physische Dasein,* p. 65.

31   Steiner: *Das Leben zwischen dem Tode und der neuren Geburt im Verhältneis zue den kosmischen Tatsachen,* p. 58.

32   Steiner: *Das Geheimnis des Todes,* p. 121.

33   Ibid., p. 28.

34   Steiner: *Das Leben zwischen dem Tode und der neuen Begurt im Verhältnis zu den kosmischen Tatscachen,* p. 168.

35   Rudolf Steiner: *Geschichtliche Notwendigkeit und Freiheit. Scvhicksalseinwirkungen aus der Welt der Toten,* p. 55.

36   Steiner: *Okkulte Untersuchungen über das Leben swischen Tod und neuer Geburt,* p. 332.

37   Ibid., p. 116. On December 31, 1905, Rudolf Steiner wrote to his esoteric pupil Paula Stryczek, who had turned to him for advice after the death of Anna Wagner (1847-1905): Dear Miss Stryczek, Let me say this to you on the occasion of this unhappy event. When a person dear to us crosses into the other worlds, it is especially important to send our thoughts and feelings without in any way giving the impression that we want her back, which would make life difficult for her in the new spheres she is entering. What we should send into her worlds is not our own *sorrow,* but our *love* for her. Don't misunderstand me; I do not mean that we must be hardened or indifferent. But it should be possible for us to look toward the dead person and think, "May my love accompany you and surround you." According to my insights, such feelings give wings to the dead person, whereas the feelings of many

mourners (such as, 'Oh, if you were only still here with us') become obstacles in her path. This is a general suggestion about how we ought to direct our feelings in such cases. In this particular case, let me advise you to take up some thoughts based on ancient occult traditions, although they are not yet fully accessible to me in good German. In inner stillness, say them to yourself three times a day, one of which should be immediately before you fall asleep, so you take them with you into the spiritual world. Ideally, you should fall asleep with the thoughts: *May the offering of my love envelop you, cooling all heat, warming all cold. May my gift of light carry you upward on wings of love.* It is important to have the right feelings when it comes to the words "heat" and "cold." They do not mean physical heat and cold but rather warmth and coolness of feeling, although it is not easy for someone still embedded in the physical sheath to get an idea of what these qualities signify to the disembodied. A recently deceased person must first become aware that the astral element is still effective even though it cannot make use of physical tools. Many of our earthly aspirations are fulfilled by physical tools, and now those tools are no longer there. The soul experiences not having physical organs as something similar to—but only *similar* to—a burning thirst. That is the strong sensation of "heat" upon becoming disembodied. The same applies to what our will wants to do: It is accustomed to using physical organs it no longer has. On the soul level, this "deprivation" is comparable to a sensation of cold. Intervention by the living can be especially helpful with regard to these feelings, which are not exclusively the results of an individual life but are related to the mysteries of incarnation. That is why it is possible for us to come to the aid of a disembodied friend. There is still one more thing that I would ask of you: Precede the above sentences by directing a few thoughts toward Mr. Wagner. Their content should be something like this: "Her true love surrounded you until now and continues to surround you, unchanged. May she continue to hold you, in strength of spirit, just as she illumined you through her visible presence." I wanted to write to you today, but physical work obscures spiritual experience, and at the moment I have so much work to do on the physical plane that I cannot give you anything more *specific* than this general advice. Of course you should feel free to share these lines with anyone you see fit. I hope that many hearts will turn toward this personality who is so dear to us. Please give my best regards to our dear Doctor and be assured of the same for yourself. Yours truly, Dr. Rudolf Steiner. (In: Rudolf Steiner: *Zur Geschichte und aus den Inhalten der ersten Abteilung der Esoterischen Schule 1904 bis 1914*, p. 101ff.).

38   Steiner: *Unsere Toten*, p. 200f.

39   Steiner: *Geschichtliche Notwendigkeit und Freiheit. Schicksalseinwirkungen aus der Welt der Toten*, p. 55f.

40   Rudolf Steiner: *Der Tod als Lebenswandlung*, p. 20.

41   Steiner: *Das Geheimnis des Todes*, p. 199.

42   "It is certainly so that even what we receive inwardly stems from outer spiritual influences. We can account for these spiritual influences concretely and in detail." (Rudolf Steiner: *Die Verbindung zwischen Lebenden und Toten*, p. 47). Cf. note 43.

43   Ibid., p. 214. For an example of how a deceased individual advanced Rudolf Steiner's spiritual scientific research, see Steiner's lecture of October 1, 1913 in Bergen (in: *Okkulte Undersuchungen über das Leben zwischen Tod und neuer Geburt*, p. 339ff.). In his lectures of May 10, May 12, and July 14, 1914 (in: *Wie erwirbt man sich Verständnis für die geistige Welt?* and *Christus und die menschliche Seele*, respectively), Rudolf Steiner gives the further example of the "assistance" of Maria von Strauch-Spettini (d. 1904) in realizing the Mystery Dramas in Munich in 1910-1913. And in Berlin on May 12, 1914, Steiner said: "Early on in our spiritual-scientific activity, at the very beginning, we were visited by a personality who not only developed a profoundly inward and deeply felt connection to our spiritual-scientific teachings in the form in which they were necessarily presented at that early stage but was also totally imbued with a wonderfully refined artistic sensibility. In the truest sense of the word, this

was an objectively likeable personality. She rapidly absorbed all the spiritual-scientific teachings that could be made available at that time. Then—still in the early years of our work—she left the physical plane. In the years that followed, out of the subconscious depths accessible to human souls who have passed through the portal of death, this person's individuality worked to merge what she had received from our spiritual-scientific teachings with her artistic sensibility. I might say that it was possible to trace the development of a spirit body in which these two forces worked together: on the one hand fruitful spiritual-scientific views, on the other her likeable, energetic, and insightful artistic sensibility. Years passed in this way, and then increasingly often, as our tasks in Munich became apparent, it happened that when I faced decisions related to more detailed inner aspects of our presentations in Munich, I knew that this individuality was looking down on everything going on there. Since the strengths we acquire in the physical world come from the physical world, of course it is not true that we learn what we need to do from such beings. We must find the ability within ourselves. But inasmuch as her warm, inward participation in our cause and the protective rays of her spiritual eye flowed into what I had to do, I felt imbued with energy and blessed by the forces that emanate from such an individuality. Such examples show us how a soul that has passed through the portal of death is gradually transformed into a being who works with us here on the physical plane. When we begin to sense this assistance consciously, we experience such a being as a protective, strengthening spirit acting on behalf of something that must be done here but relates to the spiritual world. We then tackle this work on the assumption that a being hovering in the spiritual worlds is serving as the protective spirit for this work." (Steiner: *Wie erwirbt man sich Verständnis für die geistige Welt?*, p. 71f.).

44 Steiner: *Der Tod als Lebenswandlung*, p. 30f.
45 Steiner: *Okkulte Untersuchungen über das Leben zwischen Tod und neuer Geburt*, p. 331.

46   Ibid., p. 131f.

47   Steiner: *Unsere Toten*, p. 11f.

48   Ibid., p. 150.

49   Ibid., p. 21.

50   Ibid., p. 332.

51   Ibid., p. 64.

52   Ibid., p. 235.

53   Ibid., p. 57.

54   Ibid., p. 72.

55   Cf. ibid., p. 282ff.

56   Ibid., p. 188.

57   Ibid., p. 187.

58   Ibid., p. 249.

59   Ibid., p. 199.

60   Cf. ibid., pp. 220 and 234, among others.

61   Ibid., p. 103.

62   Ibid., p. 234.

63   Ibid., pp. 225 and 241.

64   Ibid., p. 259.

65   Ibid., p. 263.

66   Ibid., p. 177.

67   Ibid., p. 275.

68   Ibid., p. 256f.

69   Ibid., p. 262.

70   Ibid., p. 75.

71   Ibid., p. 106.

72   Ibid., pp. 122-129.

73   Ibid., p. 115.

74   Steiner: *Das Geheimnis des Todes*, p. 38f.

75   Ibid., p. 40.

76   Ibid., p. 116.

77   Ibid., p. 114f.

78   Ibid., p. 116.

79   Ibid., p. 117.

80   According to Rudolf Steiner, an inherent part of any memo-
      rial address or of accompanying the deceased is to support
      the departed soul in the early stages of self-discovery in the

spiritual world (ibid., p. 91). It is important, says Steiner, to "help strengthen the self-awareness of the deceased, the departed" (ibid., p. 361) by concretely presenting the soul with the "image" of its own being (ibid., p.362). On June 17, 1914, in Düsseldorf, Rudolf Steiner spoke of the emergence and meaning of his cremation verses: "Why this inspiration or intuition to call out to the dead with something related to their being? Their life after death shows us why. Turning to them in this way helps them strengthen their forces of self-awareness. By speaking immediately after their deaths (when their consciousness has not yet awakened) of traits they sense in themselves, we send them some of the strength they need to gradually become able to view the moment of death, when their entire being as it developed between birth and death seems concentrated. Right after death, it is a help to the dead to send them something that reminds them of traits, experiences, etc., that were once theirs. It promotes forces of self-awareness. Those with the clairvoyant ability to put themselves in the place of a deceased soul sense that soul's urge to hear about its character, its actions, or its most important traits during life." (Ibid., p. 331).

81   Three months later, on July 17 in Düsseldorf, without giving her name, Rudolf Steiner reported additional details about the development of Lina Grosheintz's consciousness after death, especially in connection to Easter. He spoke again of his own experiences with his deceased fellow-anthroposophist, saying, "Of course if I would describe everything such souls experience, there would be much to report about the time that then begins for a soul [after laying aside the etheric body]. I only have described parts of this process, and naturally, in the context of our movement, one of the most important aspects is the soul's activity after death, especially when the soul in question has been as close to us as this one. And so it happened that the first opportunity to observe this soul as she reoriented her consciousness came in her participation in our gatherings. Yes, she really participated in our gatherings. Her participation was fully developed at the Dornach Easter

celebration this year, where we made a particular effort to explain the depth of the idea of this festival to our dear friends in Dornach. This soul was present; she took part. Just as she once took part with inner warmth, she now participated as a soul. And she wanted to express herself just as many in physical bodies also feel the need to speak about what they have received. She wanted to express herself, and the remarkable thing about it is that she again did so in words we could understand. She chose words that described how she was living, especially in connection with what she had experienced during the Easter lecture, so in effect the lecture was complemented by remarks from one who had passed through death. This addition that emerged from consciousness was: *In human souls I will guide / Spirit feeling, that it may willingly / awaken the Easter-Word in hearts; // With human spirits I will think / Soul warmth, that they may strongly / feel the Risen One.* You see, she wants to continue to work with her associates in our spiritual-scientific movement. She wants to dedicate herself to allowing the Easter-Word to awaken in their hearts, as the Easter lecture attempted to do, so that what we call the Risen One can be sensed in the right way. What emerged in three additional lines, however, was very significant as well as especially beautiful and deeply moving. In that Easter lecture and in many other lectures around the same time, I had attempted repeatedly (as I have often done) to draw attention to the importance of spiritual science not only for earthly life but for the entire world. It is possible for one who has passed through the portal of death to experience everything we do here in spiritual science. That is why I advise so many of you with loved ones who have passed through the portal of death to read aloud to them or tell them about spiritual-scientific teachings, because anything formulated in the words of spiritual science has significance not only for souls living in physical bodies but also for disembodied souls. For them, such words are like the spiritual air or water of life itself or—to put it differently—they perceive light through us here below. For us, initially, this light is symbolic, because we hear words and receive them into our souls as thoughts, but the dead really see this light as spirit light. Now it is very significant that this soul, who had heard me say this often, positively insisted on saying that she understood it, and that it really is so! Her words in this connection were: *The earthly flame of spirit knowledge / shines bright into death's semblance./ The self becomes World-Eye, World-Ear.* For the soul, this is a fact. What she means by *earthly flame* is that what you say down below shines upward like a flame. Why does she say *death's semblance?* If you think about it, you will find out. Because she always heard us call the world maya, illusion, she says that on earth she lived in the illusion of the senses and now she also finds herself in an illusion through which she must see the reality. And then she confirms, *the self becomes World-Eye, World-Ear.* She means that the entire Self now becomes a powerful sense organ, an organ of perception for the whole cosmos. In this very beautiful way, the dead person reveals how she becomes conscious of the truth of what spiritual science says. Characteristically, this soul wanted to express herself immediately after death, saying, now I have come so far that what I learned on earth is revealed to me as true." (*Das Geheimnis des Todes*, p. 334ff.).

82   Steiner: *Unsere Toten*, p. 116.
83   Ibid., p. 120f.
84   Steiner: *Das Geheimnis des Todes*, p. 88.
85   Ibid., p. 112.
86   Ibid., p. 63.
87   Ibid., p. 113, italics added.
88   Steiner: *Das Geheimnis des Todes*, p. 90.
89   Ibid., p. 35f.
90   Ibid., p. 44.
91   Ibid.
92   Ibid., p. 47.
93   Ibid., p. 94.
94   Ibid.
95   Ibid., p. 95.

96   Ibid., p. 365.

97   Steiner: *Unsere Toten*, p. 240.

98   Ibid., p. 301.

99   Ibid., p. 272.

100 Steiner: *Das Geheimnis des Todes*, p. 108.

101 Ibid., p. 267.

102 Ibid., p. 223.

103 Rudolf Steiner: *Die Verbindung zwischen Lebenden und Toten*, p. 46.

104 Steiner: *Das Geheimnis des Todes*, p. 42.

105 Ibid., p. 110.

106 Rudolf Steiner: *Die Geistige Hintergründe des Ersten Weltkrieges*, p. 76.

107 Steiner: *Das Geheimnis des Todes*, p. 225.

108 In: Erika Beltle and Kurt Vierl, eds.: *Erinnerungen an Rudolf Steiner*, p. 186f.

109 Rudolf Steiner: *Der Dornacher Bau als Wharzeichen geschichtlichen Werdens und künstlerischer Umwandlungsimpulse*, p. 18.

110 Ibid., p. 19.

111 Ibid., p. 18. By the previous day (October 9, 1914), two days after the child's death, Theo's mother had already written to his father about the accident and what followed, as well as about what Rudolf Steiner and Marie von Sivers had said: "That night was terrible. Around midnight his body was recovered. It was heartrending for everyone; everybody was up and no one got any sleep. Dr. Steiner broke the news to me gently, saying that there was no space for his big spirit in that little body, and that I might console myself with the thought that he was too good for this earth, that everyone loved him and would always preserve the memory of his radiant little face. Miss von Sivers said that now that he was free to transcend himself, he would be a pillar of strength for us and for the building, because he had a big spirit that he could not put to use here in the physical world." (Quoted in Lex Bos: "Theo Faiss." In: *Mitteilungen aus der anthroposophischen Arbeit in Deutschland*. Vol. 41, Issue 3, No. 161. Michaelmas 1987, p. 209f.).

112 Rudolf Steiner: *Zufall, Notwendigkeit und Vorsehung. Imaginative Erkenntnis und Vorgänge nach dem Tode*, p. 116.
113 Ibid., p. 136.
114 Cf. Steiner: *Das Geheimnis des Todes*, p. 286, and *Zufall, notwendigkeit und Vorsehung. Imaginative Erkenntnis und Vorgänge nach dem Tode*, p. 117f.
115 Steiner: *Das Geheimnis des Todes*, p. 43. In this lecture (of February 2, 1915), Rudolf Steiner points out that the etheric forces of Theo Faiss, which were incorporated into the aura of the building, possessed not only a childlike quality but also attributes of previous incarnations. In other words, they had obviously been prepared for this task: "This etheric body, woven through with all the delicate, beautiful forces developed in childhood, is also filled with forces that come from earlier incarnations." (Ibid.).
116 Ibid., p. 62.
117 Steiner: *Zufall, Notwendigkeit und Vorsehung. Imaginative Erkenntnis und Vorgänge nach dem Tode*, p. 117.
118 Steiner: *Das Geheimnis des Todes*, p. 282.
119 Ibid., p. 282f.
120 Ibid., p. 43.
121 Ibid., p. 225.
122 Ibid., p. 111.
123 Ibid., p. 175.
124 Steiner. *Zufall, Notwendigkeit und Vorsehung. Imaginative Erkenntnis und Vorgänge nach dem Tode*, p. 22.
125 Steiner: *Das Geheimnis des Todes*, p. 290.
126 Ibid., p. 225.
127 Ibid., p. 286.
128 Ibid., p. 269.
129 Ibid., p. 287.
130 Steiner: *Unsere Toten*, p. 169.
131 Ibid., p. 151.
132 Ibid., p. 172.
133 Ibid., p. 159.
134 Ibid.
135 Ibid., p. 175.

136 Ibid., p. 169.
137 Ibid.
138 Ibid., p. 151.
139 Ibid., p. 173.
140 Ibid., p. 173f.
141 Ibid., p. 150.
142 Ibid., p. 157.
143 Ibid.
144 Ibid., p. 167.
145 Ibid., p. 157.
146 Ibid., p. 168.
147 Ibid.
148 Ibid., p. 158.
149 Ibid., p.165f.
150 Ibid., p. 177.
151 Ibid., p. 167.
152 Ibid., p. 151.
153 Ibid., p. 159.
154 Ibid.
155 Ibid., p. 160.
156 Ibid., p. 169.
157 Ibid., p. 160.
158 On the situation in Dornach in 1915, see also Peter Selg: *Marie Steiner-von Sivers. Aufbau und Zukunft des Werkes von Rudolf Steiner*. Dornach 2006, p. 117ff. and Andrei Belyi: *Geheime Aufzeichnungen. Erinnerungen an das Leben im Umkreis Rudolf Steiners (1911-1915)*. Dornach 2002, p. 147ff.
159 Steiner: *Unsere Toten*, p. 152.
160 "I recall how she came up to me in Berlin after a lecture about the Goetheanum. She gave me a meaningful look and said, 'The Johannesbau is a human being, the new human being.' And then she walked on." (Andrei Belyi: *Verwandeln des Lebens. Erinnerungen an Rudolf Steiner*. Basel 1975, p. 261).
161 Steiner: *Unsere Toten*, p. 177.
162 Ibid., p. 178f.
163 Ibid.
164 Ibid., p. 171.

165 Ibid., p. 179.
166 Ibid., p. 160.
167 Ibid., p. 161.
168 Ibid., p. 163.
169 Ibid.
170 Ibid., p. 153ff.
171 Ibid., p. 274.
172 Ibid., p. 264.
173 Ibid., p. 270.
174 Ibid.
175 Ibid.
176 Ibid., p 264.
177 Ibid., p. 266.
178 Ibid., p. 272.
179 Ibid., p. 271.
180 Ibid., p. 272.
181 Ibid., p. 264.
182 Ibid., p. 265.
183 Ibid., p. 273.
184 Ibid., p. 265.
185 Ibid., p. 274.
186 Ibid.
187 Ibid.
188 Ibid., p. 265.
189 Ibid.
190 Ibid., p. 266.
191 Cf. Peter Selg: *Mysterium cordis. Studien zu einer sakramentalen Physiologie des Herzorganes. Aristoteles, Thomas von Aquin, Rudolf Steiner.* Dornach 2006.
192 Steiner: *Unsere Toten,* p. 274f.
193 Ibid.
194 Ibid., p. 275.
195 Ibid., p. 276.
196 Ibid., p. 267f.
197 Rudolf Steiner: *Esoterische Unterweisungen für die erste Klasse der Freien Hochschule für Geisteswissenschaft am Goetheanum 1924,* Vol. 2, p. 29.

198 Steiner: *Unsere Toten*, p. 298.
199 Ibid., p. 299.
200 Ibid., italics added.
201 Cf. Peter Selg: *Die Gestalt Christi. Rudolf Steiner und die geistige Intention des zentralen Goetheanum-Kunstwerkes*. Arlesheim 2008. See also Selg: *Edith Maryon, Rudolf Steiner und die Dornacher Christus-Plastik*. Dornach 2006.
202 Steiner: *Unsere Toten*, p. 300f.
203 Ibid.
204 Ibid., p. 301f.
205 Ibid., p. 305.
206 Ibid.
207 Ibid., p. 306.
208 Ibid., p. 307.
209 Ibid., p. 314.
210 Ibid., p. 304.
211 Ibid., p. 311.
212 Ibid., p. 313.
213 Ibid.
214 Ibid., p. 314.
215 Ibid.
216 Ibid., p. 315ff.
217 A revised and expanded version of the chapter of the same name in: P. Selg: *Sterben, Tokd un geistiges Leben. Die Kondolenzbriefe Ita Wegmans und das Todesverständnis der anthroposophischen Geisteswissenschaft*. Dornach 2005, pp. 79-95.
218 Steiner: *Das Geheimnis des Todes*, p. 36.
219 Steiner: *Der Tod als Lebenswandlung*, p. 36.
220 Cf. Peter Selg: *Vom Logos menschlicher Physis. Die Entfaltung einer anthroposophischen Humanphysologie im Werk Rudolf Steiners*. Dornach 2000, pp. 352ff. See also Selg: *Quellentexte für die Wissenschaften. Band 3: Physiologische Menschenkunde*. Dornach 2004, pp. 39ff.
221 Cf. Selg: *Vom Logos menschlicher Physis* (pp. 306ff. and 428ff.) and *Quellentexte für die Wissenschaften*, pp. 247ff.
222 Rudolf Steiner: *Individuelle Gesitwesen und ihr Wirken in der Seele des Menschen*, p. 27.

223 Rudolf Steiner: *Vom Einheitsstaat zum dreigliedrigen sozialen Organismus*, p. 261.

224 Rudolf Steiner: *Drei Schritte der Anthroposophie: Philosophie, Kosmologie, Religion*, p. 73.

225 Ibid.

226 Cf. also Rudolf Steiner's explanations of the failure of the nutritive processes of the metabolic-limb system in relationship to the increasing activity of the I-organization with age. In: *Meditative Anleitungen und Betrachtungen zur Vertiefung der Heilkunst*, p. 31f.

227 Rudolf Steiner: *Menschenwerden, Weltenseele und Weltengeist 2. Teil*, p. 158ff.

228 Re: the role of disease processes in preparing for the event of death and developments that follow death, cf. Rudolf Steiner's accounts in Peter Selg: *Krankheit, Heilung und Schicksal des Menschen. Über Rudolf Steiners geisteswissenschaftliches Pathologie- und Therapieverständnis*. Dornach 2004, p. 97ff. "Present within us are disharmonies that make it impossible for us to enter the spiritual world. Perhaps the spiritual world is shrouded in fog or other obstacles are present, and we cannot take them with us into the spiritual world as they are. In such cases, illness strikes before death and frees our souls from disharmony to such an extent that we are then able to enter the spiritual world." (Steiner: *Das Geheimnis des Todes*, p. 339).

229 Rudolf Steiner: *Vor dem Tore der Theosophie*, p. 28.

230 Steiner: *Die Verbindung zwischen Lebenden und Toten*, p. 42.

231 Ibid., p. 13. For details, see also Rudolf Steiner's striking description of this experience in his lecture in Vienna on April 13, 1914. (*Inneres Wesen des Menschen und Leben zwischen Tod und Geburt*, p. 145ff.).

232 In his book *Theosophy*, Rudolf Steiner writes: "The body's own laws determine when it will die. In general, it must be said that the soul and the spirit do not leave the body but rather let it go when its forces can no longer work in ways that serve the human organization." (p. 85; compare

this passage to textual variants first made available in 2004 in a comparative review: Rudolf Steiner: *Theosophie. Die Textentwicklung der Auflagen 1904–1922 in vollständiger Lesefassung.* Rudolf Steiner Studien, Vol. IX. Dornach 2004, p. 131. In a lecture in Stuttgart on November 21, 1915, in particular, Rudolf Steiner emphasized that from the perspective of the individuality saying farewell to earthly life, the "departure" of the physical body must also be seen as the "departure" of the individuality's entire earthly surroundings. In that lecture, Steiner said: "To those who remain here in physical life, it feels as if something formerly enveloped in the physical body of the deceased is *leaving*, going away into another world. The initial perception of the deceased, however, is that of being *abandoned* by the earth's inhabitants and by his own physical body, which was the instrument of perception, thinking, feeling, and willing between birth and death. The deceased's first perception is the "departure" of his companions and associates. This perception is connected to processes we have often described, namely, that the earth itself "goes away," taking the physical body of the deceased with it. The dead person definitely has the feeling of remaining behind while the earth's movement, imperceptible during life, continues: The earth goes away, taking with it everything that once surrounded that person on earth. Now the deceased is integrated into a totally different world, a world that facilitates the perception that the bodily sheath given to him is bound to the earth and its movements. To put it very inexactly, he has the feeling of being abandoned by the earth and its spirits because he can no longer keep up with them. He remains behind in a much quieter place; he becomes integrated into a quieter world." (*Die geistigen Hintergründe des Ersten Weltkrieges*, p. 94f.).

233 Steiner, *Die Verbindung zwischen Lebenden und Toten*, p. 13f.
234 Ibid., p. 14.
235 Cf. Selg, *Vom Logos menschlicher Physis*, p. 122ff.
236 Steiner, *Die Verbindung zwischen Lebenden und Toten*, p. 14.

237 Rudolf Steiner, *Nordische und mitteleuropäische Geistimpulse*, p. 75f.

238 Steiner: *Zufall, Notwendigkeit und Vorsehung. Imaginative Erkenntnis und Vorgänge nach dem Tode*, p. 125.

239 Rudolf Steiner, *Schicksalsbildung und Leben nach dem Tode*, p. 21.

240 In Düsseldorf on June 17, 1915, Rudolf Steiner emphasized that looking back on the experience of death and thus also on the departure of the physical body is the "most alive" and "brightest impression" the human individuality receives on the *entire* developmental path between death and rebirth. (*Das Geheimnis des Todes*, p. 327).

241 Rudolf Steiner often accentuated the majesty and beauty of this moment when he described its importance, but in his Dornach lecture of February 2, 1915, he described for the first time the light-filled, sun-related quality of warmth it bestowed on the journey after death, saying, "From the perspective of the living, death appears as a dissolution, as something that elicits slight fear and horror. From the other side of the threshold, death appears as the supremely light-filled beginning of spiritual experience, as the soul's greatest source of warmth in life between death and rebirth, as something profoundly positive to look back on repeatedly." (*Wege der geistigen Erkenntnis und der Erneuerung der künstlerischen Weltanschauung*, p. 81). Not quite three weeks later, in Bremen, Rudolf Steiner spoke of the "sun point" of the moment of death in the context of the development of consciousness after death: "After death, consciousness is dulled because we are initially flooded with consciousness by the review of life that happens right after death, although not in cases of suicide. It is one of the most beautiful and exalted experiences we know." (Steiner: *Das Geheimnis des Todes*, p. 63). In dealing with the theme of the spiritual *sunlike* quality of the moment of death and its significance for I-consciousness after death, it should be noted that—according to Rudolf Steiner's accounts of August 28, 1917 in Berlin—there are deep connections between the Mystery of Golgotha (or the

Christ's earthly experience of death and overcoming it: *"In Christ, death becomes life"*) and the development of human consciousness. The fact that the Christ being passed through earthly death, says Steiner, permanently altered the make-up of human consciousness; increasingly, since Golgotha, the human individuality's moment of death is becoming increasingly able to activate organs for future cognition of the Christ: "In which moment do we hope for a concentrated understanding of the Christ? In the moment of death! In that moment, all the forces that maintained our consciousness throughout life are present. In the moment of death, we are capable of receiving the essential mystery of our consciousness and thus also the Christ-Impulse." (*Menschliche und menschheitliche Entwicklungswahrheiten. Das Karma des Materialismus*, p. 289). Steiner continues, explaining that the "moment of having died" creates the necessary conditions for a future cognitive/beholding encounter with the Christ on the journey after death: "We can only understand what we encounter in death if the organ for understanding it is freed up. In other words, the moment of death provides the conditions for uniting with the Christ, but only after we are released from the etheric body are the I and astral body— which provide the organs of understanding in this case— capable of beholding what has united with us." (Ibid.).

242 Steiner: *Die Verbindung zwischen Lebenden und Toten*, p. 42; italics added.

243 Ibid., p. 72.

244 Steiner: *Die geistigen Gründe des Ersten Weltkrieges*, p. 99f.

245 Steiner: *Zufall, Notwendigkeit und Vorsehen. Imaginative Erkenntnis und Vorgänge nach dem Tode*, p. 134f.

246 Steiner: *Geheimnis des Todes*, p. 327f.

247 Steiner: *Die Verbindung zwischen Lebenden und Toten*, p. 72.

248 Steiner: *Die geistigen Gründe des Ersten Weltkrieges*, p. 99.

249 Steiner: *Das Geheimnis des Todes*, p. 35.

250 Ibid., p. 87.

251 Steiner: *Wege der geistigen Erkenntnis und der Erneuerung der künstlerischen Weltanschauung*, p. 81f.

252 Steiner: *Das Geheimnis des Todes*, p. 91; italics added.
253 Ibid., p. 114.
254 According to Rudolf Steiner, the physical body, "The most marvelous structure that exists anywhere in the world" (*Die Verblndung Zwischen Lebenden und Toten*, p. 70) unites with earthly existence at interment, returning that part of its being that comes from the earth to the earth's "elements" and "substances": *"The earthly remains of a human being form a whole with the entire earth"* (Letter to Countess Pauline von Kalckreuth, February 4, 1916. In: *Mitteilungen aus der anthroposophischen Arbeit in Deutschland*. Christmas 1969, p. 279). Burning or decay of the corpse differ only in their temporal structure, not in their qualitative outcomes: Although the length of time may vary, the physical body is ultimately completely transformed into heat: "Even if it takes centuries—or in the case of the skeletal system, possibly even millennia—the last remnants of the material body are transformed into heat" (*Die Verbindung zwischen Lebenden und Toten*, p. 13). The physical body and the heat it generates are incorporated and transformed into the earth, and all of the processes of the individual's biographical development are inscribed on this heat. In 1919, Rudolf Steiner had this to say about the significance of incorporating this heat into the organism of the earth: "These fructifying suprasensible forces maintain the process of the earth's evolution. Without human corpses, therefore, the earth would have been dead long ago." (*Allgemeine Menschenkunde als Grundlage der Pädagogik*, p. 54; cf. also Rudolf Steiner: *Soziales Verständnis aus geisteswissenschaftlicher Erkenntnis*, p. 60ff. and *Der innere Aspekt des sozialen Rätsels*, p. 149f.).
255 Steiner: *Dei Verbindung zwischen Lebenden und Toten*, p. 73. As Rudolf Steiner described in his lecture of February 22, 1916, the spiritual forces of the physical body—unlike its earthly aspect, which is in the process of being transformed into heat—unite with the cosmos to form the actual surroundings of the excarnating individuality. Leading up to the experience of "emptiness," Rudolf Steiner says in that

lecture in Leipzig: "What about our physical body, that most marvelous of all the structures that exist in the world? Only what it received from the earth returns to the earth. Where is the rest, once we have passed through the portal of death? That remainder, pulling away from the part that sinks into the earth as the result of decay or cremation, is absorbed into the entire universe. If you think of everything you can imagine in the earth's surroundings, with all the planets and fixed stars, and imagine it as spiritualized as possible, you will have the place where our spiritual aspect is. Only part of this spiritual aspect is separated out as heat and incorporated into the earth. Our own heat, our inner warmth, remains with the earth. All other spiritual elements of the physical body, however, are carried out into space, into the entire cosmos. When we human beings leave our physical bodies, where do we go? What do we submerge into? At death, with the speed of lightning, we submerge into all of the suprasensible forces that shape the physical body. Imagine all the structural forces that have been working on your physical body since the time of Old Saturn. Imagine them expanding to infinity and preparing the place for you to live between death and a new birth. Between birth and death, all of these forces are compressed into the space enclosed by our skin. In this physical body, which is so small relative to the world as a whole, we have a microcosm, an entire world that is simply rolled up into this small space, if I may put it in rather prosaic terms. At death, it unrolls and fills the entire world, with the exception of one small space that always remains empty. We spend the time between death and a new birth in the whole cosmos of suprasensible forces that underlie our physical body here, but there is one space that remains empty. That is the space inside our skin that we occupy here in the physical world." (*Die Verbilndung zwischen Lebenden und Toten*, p. 70f./73).

256   Ibid., p. 73.
257   Ibid., p. 43; italics added.
258   Ibid., p. 73.
259   Ibid.

260   "I have thought about this a great deal, and in attempting to
describe how the etheric body is assimilated into the etheric
world, the best term I can find is "Inbindung," tying in.
The physical body falls apart, the etheric body is "tied in."
What we have contributed to it is tied in or connected to the
entire etheric world—hence "tying in" as opposed to "falling
apart." (*Zufall, Notwendigkeit und Vorsehung. Imaginative
Erkenntnis und Vorgänge nach dem Tode*, p. 126).

261   The separation of the etheric body from the human organization as a whole and its successive dissolution into the etheric
cosmos (see below) is a necessary step in the dissociation of
the physical and etheric bodies. As Rudolf Steiner repeatedly
explained, the physical body is what keeps the etheric sphere
of formative forces "within limits" (*Anthroposophische
Menschenerkenntnis und Medizin*, p. 209) in the human
being and overcomes its centrifugal orientation in favor of a
unifying tendency that allows the body to assume form: "If
we were to lose our physical body for even a moment during
life, an expanding force would immediately give the etheric
body the tendency to dissolve into the entire cosmos. During
life, the etheric body is held together only by being in a
physical body" (*Geistige Zusammenhänge in der Gestaltung
des menschichen Organismus*, p. 160). According to Rudolf
Steiner, this centrifugal orientation is an expression of the
fact that the etheric body is essentially a cosmic entity; even
during its time of earthly individualization, it remains inti
mately and inseparably connected to the etheric forces of
the cosmos: "What works in the astral body has been inter-
woven with the human being out of the etheric nature of the
cosmos and can never separate completely from the cosmos.
Cosmic etheric activity extends into the human organization; this internal human continuation is the human etheric
organism" (*Drei Schritte der Anthroposophie: Philosophie,
Kosmologie, Religion*, p. 74). After earthly death, the etheric
body of formative forces escapes from its human-like form,
which is essentially achieved through the organized forces of
the physical body. Against this background, Rudolf Steiner

said on February 6, 1915, in Dornach: "When the moment of death is described objectively, the etheric body is described as rising up and out like a cloud. As it does so, it initially still presents the shape of the physical body with its arms and other appendages, but then it gradually dissolves in the more spiritual forces that work in from the cosmos. This is a transformation, a metamorphosis, a transition." (*Wege der geistigen Erkenntnis und der Erneuerung der künstlerischen Weltanschauung*, p. 109).

262 Cf. Selg: *Vom Logos menschlicher Physis*, p. 103ff., 224ff., 286ff., and 548ff.

263 Rudolf Steiner: *Die Theosophie des Rosenkreuzers*, p. 38. This description was given in a lecture in Munich in May of 1907. Eight years later, Steiner gave further details, emphasizing that the "tableau of memories" is centered on the human "I." He emphasized its crucial importance in self-development after death and downplayed its "objective" (neutral) character somewhat. On November 16, 1915, he said in Berlin: "In the time right after death, we see a great tableau of the life just passed. It runs for several days, but always as if the whole of our past life is present to us at once, as if spread out in front of us in a grand panorama. When we look more closely, however, it turns out that what we can observe during these days of review has a specific focus: We see our life from the perspective of the 'I'; the tableau emphasizes everything in which the 'I' was involved. For example, if we see our connection to another person, we see it in the context of the fruits it bore for us. In other words, we do not see these things totally objectively; we see primarily their consequences for us. The 'I' is always in the center. This focus is totally necessary, because these days of seeing what yielded fruit for the 'I' are the source of the inner strength and energy we will need in order to hold fast to the thought of the individual 'I' throughout life between death and a new birth" (*Schicksalsbildung und Leben nach dem Tode*, p. 20). Two weeks later, in Munich, Rudolf Steiner again emphasized the I-focused and centering aspect of the

etheric "tableau of memories," saying that the individual who has passed through the portal of death "senses this tableau of life as a part of her Self. Initially, the tableau is her entire world. In these days after death, we do not distinguish between World and Self. The two flow together; self-experience *is* the world" (*Mitteleurope zwischen Ost und West,* p. 83f.). In the same lecture (and even more clearly than in his description of November 16, 1915), it is obvious that Steiner was defining the experience of consciousness "in the moment of having died" more broadly to include the tableau of memories that follows it. In a certain respect, that is, he consolidated the two experiences with respect to their importance as the foundation of self-experience after death. He said, "As spiritual beings, having passed through the portal of death, we continue to live in the stream of time and look back on what we experienced during death. In this process, the soul as it continues to move on repeatedly encounters its life's panorama in spiritual memory. Here in earthly life, I-consciousness is kindled by the encounter of the 'I' with the physical body. Similarly, after death, I-consciousness is kindled by looking back on our most recent earthly life. That is how we experience I-consciousness between death and a new birth" (Ibid., p. 87). "Seeing the [tableau] is the point of origin for maintaining the 'I' throughout life between death and rebirth. This experience strengthens and energizes the soul so that it knows 'I am an I!' for the duration of the time between death and rebirth." (Ibid., p. 42f.).

264 Steiner: *Die Verbindung zwischen Lebenden und Toten,* pp. 44 & 74.

265 "We can call this 'laying aside the etheric body,' but in fact it is the constant growth and expansion of memories, which lose the third dimension to become two dimensional, that is, completely pictorial." (*Initiations-Erkenntnis,* p. 158f.).

266 Rudolf Steiner: *Die Geheiwissenschaft im Umriss,* p. 95. *Cf.* also *Inneres Wesen des Menschen und Leben zwischen Tod und neuer Geburt,* p. 51.

267 Steiner: *Die Verbindung zwischen Lebenden und Toten,* p. 75.

268   In Stuttgart on November 23, 1915, Rudolf Steiner spoke about the soul-spiritual *activity* that becomes evident in this process, shaping the individuality's existence after the physical body is laid aside: "The first manifestation in soul life [after physical corporeality falls away] might be called a reversal of feeling with regard to life. Here on earth, we have the feeling that our life comes to us from outside, that we live as a result of life forces provided by the earth from outside. Now the earth moves away from us, so to speak, taking these forces with it. The immediate result of this abandonment is the feeling that enlivening energy is now welling up within us. The first manifestation, therefore, is the perception that we are self-enlivening. It marks the transition to a certain degree of activity—*you* are enlivening what you now are; you are in your Self—in place of your former passivity. What we formerly called 'the world' has moved away from us. The element in which we now live, filling it completely, creates enlivening forces within itself; it enlivens itself. The concrete result is what I have often called the panorama of life—the stream of images of everything we experienced between birth and death. Images of that lifetime appear to the soul. A mighty, self-engendering dream of the entire most recent life between birth and death emerges as if from the point where we are now. This image would be just an ebbing dream if we had not achieved the awareness that our own bodily envelope has freed itself from the spirit and soul. Through the strength of this consciousness, the dream image becomes alive. What would otherwise remain only a dark world of dream images ebbing away is enlivened; it becomes a living world, a living panorama of life. We ourselves are the source for enlivening what initially appears as a dream. That is what we experience immediately after death.

All this happens while we are scarcely aware of having left our former consciousness behind. It is as if something in the center of our being is stirring, expanding, and escaping from the life to which we once submitted passively. Between birth and death, we did not know that thoughts—which seemed simply to ebb and flow like dreams of the 'I'—are alive, but now we know it. We extricate ourselves from that former life, which came from outside, and find our way into our own existence. Something that formerly came from outside is now welling up within, and we experience the significance of this inversion. What we knew before was not life but the image of life, but now it works from within, taking hold of our ideation and thinking." (*Die geistingen Hintergründe des Ersten Weltkrieges*, p. 95f.).

269 In 1924, Rudolf Steiner wrote that the "tableau of memories" encompasses in image form all of life's contents that "entered memory during life's journey in the form of imageless thoughts or remained unnoticed by earthly consciousness but nonetheless made a subconscious impression on the soul." (*Anthroposophische Leitsätze*, p. 25).

270 Steiner: *Inneres Wesen des Menschen und Leben zwischen Tod und neuer Geburt*, p. 52.

271 Steiner: *Die Verbindung zwischen Lebenden und Toten*, p. 15. In Oslo on May 16, 1923, Rudolf Steiner spoke about perceiving the etheric body of thoughts and its subsequent union with the cosmic etheric world (see below): "For two to four days after death, we have the feeling of consisting entirely of thoughts, but these thoughts are breaking up. As a thought-being, the human being grows larger and larger, finally dissolving into the cosmos " (*Menschenwesen, Menschenschicksal und Welt-Entwickelung*, p. 18).

272 Steiner: *Die Verbindung zwischen Lebenden und Toten*, p. 32.

273 Ibid., p. 182.

274 In a lecture in Leipzig on February 22, 1916 (ibid., p. 76f), Rudolf Steiner mentioned that the higher hierarchies work with the etheric forces and contents of human biographies. Seven years later, in Penmaenmawr, he said: "If we think good thoughts, we surrender them to the cosmos after death. If we think bad thoughts, we also surrender them to the cosmos when we die. In an earthly existence, a human being develops not only as an independent being but also

as a being the gods themselves are working on in order to guide the cosmos from one epoch to the next. The thoughts the gods must incorporate into the cosmos are formulated in the thoughts and reflections of individual human lives. Our lives are the nursery where the gods cultivate the thoughts they need for world development. They constantly make use of such thoughts, incorporating them into their cosmos as actual force-impulses." (*Initiations-Erkenntnis*, p. 160).

275 Steiner: : *Zufall, Notwendigkeit und Vorsehung. Imaginative Erkenntnis und Vorgänge nach dem Tode*, p. 128.

276 Rudolf Steiner spoke repeatedly about how the etheric life-tableau developed and then faded over a period of days. In Stuttgart on June 21, 1923, he sketched the entire process in these words: "All at once the earthly life just past confronts the soul that has just freed itself completely from the physical body and etheric body in passing through the portal of death. This process takes place over several days after the physical body has been laid aside while the etheric body slowly dissolves into the general world ether. During this time, the soul's impression of an overview of the last earthly life is initially living and clearly defined. Then it gradually becomes weaker and weaker but also increasingly cosmic at the same time, until finally, after several days, it melts away completely." (*Die menschliche Seele in ihrem Zusammenhang mit göttliche-geistigen Individualitäten. Die Verinnerlichung der Jahresfeste*, p. 57f.).

277 Steiner: *Die Verbindung zwischen Lebenden und Toten*, p. 15. As Rudolf Steiner emphasized in Berlin on February 10, 1914, the ongoing experience of the individual human etheric body as it is transformed and incorporated into the etheric cosmos is the "main thing we see" during life immediately after death. Specifically, Steiner said: "It belongs to the destiny of our soul—that is, of our astral body and 'I', which make up the soul in the spiritual world—to behold what we ourselves have produced in the destiny of our etheric body, which can no longer be changed after it separates from the physical body. In fact, this is the main thing we

see after death. In the sensory world, we saw clouds, mountains, and so on; the comparable background after death is what we ourselves incorporated into our etheric body as the consequences of our soul's constitution and attitudes. As the etheric body dissolves, this background becomes ever larger, like the firmament against which everything else appears. Part of our destiny after death, therefore, is to behold the destiny of the etheric body." (*Aus der Akasha-Chronik*, p. 201).

278 Steiner: *Die Verbindung zwischen Lebenden und Toten*, p. 76.

279 Steiner: *Drei Schritte der Anthroposophy. Philosophie, Kosmologie, Religion.* p. 74.

280 In Karlsruhe on October 7, 1911, Rudolf Steiner spoke for the first time about this encounter with the active Christ-being as the future "lord of karma" or "karmic judge." He also emphasized the importance of this spirit-experience for the development of earthly conscience. After describing how the Christ is assuming the role of karmic judge in present times, Steiner said: "This is a fact that works into the physical world, on the physical plane: Human beings will develop a feeling for how, in everything we do, we create something for which we are accountable to the Christ. This feeling, which will develop very naturally in the course of humankind's evolution, will be transformed and flood the soul with a light that gradually begins to emanate from individuals. This light will increasingly illumine the figure of the Christ in the etheric world. As this feeling develops, it will assume greater importance than any abstract thinking. The more this thinking develops in the next few centuries, the more visible the etheric figure of the Christ will become. (*Von Jesus zu Christus*, p. 80).

Twelve years later, in the Hague on November 13, 1923, without explicitly naming the Christ-being, Rudolf Steiner emphasized that leaving the physical body behind and the subsequent dissolution of the etheric formative forces entailed a meeting of the deceased with the *"cosmic archetypal image"* of the human being in the etheric: "The cosmic archetypal image inscribed in the etheric is what we then behold. During earthly life, it was anchored in our own etheric body, but we did not perceive it. It exists on earth in our physical being, but we do not perceive it then. After death, however, we do perceive what is present in the human form, present in us." Regarding the development of human conscience, Rudolf Steiner continues: "The image we then see immediately becomes radiant, and its radiating forces have very specific consequences. It behaves like any radiant body, but on the etheric level. The sun is physically radiant, but this cosmic image of the human being is spiritually radiant, and because it is a spiritual image, its power to illuminate is also different. Here in earthly life, someone who has done good or bad deeds can stand in the sun for ever so long, but sunlight illuminates only his hair, and so on, not his good and bad deeds, as qualities. The radiant image of our own form, which we perceive in the spiritual world after passing through death, radiates a spiritual light that now illumines our moral deeds. After death, therefore, we encounter in this cosmic image something that illuminates our own moral deeds. It was hidden in us during earthly life, but spoke quietly to us as our conscience. Now, after death, we perceive it objectively. We recognize this image as our Self; it must be with us after death. This image of ours is an implacable judge. It does not conveniently forgive our sins and highlight our good deeds. It is an implacable judge and shines a clear light on what our actions were worth. Conscience itself becomes a cosmic impulse that works outside us after death." (*Der übersinnliche Mensch, anthroposophisch erfasst*, p. 75f.).

In his lecture in Berlin on February 10, 1914, in the context of presentations on the "Fifth Gospel," Rudolf Steiner stressed that for appropriately prepared souls, observing the individual etheric body as it is transformed and subsumed into the etheric cosmos is associated with perceiving Christological forces for the future in the etheric. (Cf. *Aus der Akasha-Chronik*, pp. 202ff.).

281 Steiner: *Die Verbindung zwischen Lebenden und Toten,* p. 44.
282 Ibid., p. 45.
283 With regard to "laying aside" the etheric body, increasing self-cognition and strength of will, and cognition of the spiritual world, see also Rudolf Steiner's explanations in his lecture in Cologne on June 19, 1915. (*Das Geheimnis des Todes,* in particular, pp. 357ff.).
284 "From now on, the etheric body with which we were connected and which we formerly considered our inner aspect is outside us. It becomes ever larger, weaving itself into the fabric of the spiritual world we have now entered. ("Weaving" is actually the most accurate word here.) The only part of this spiritual world it does not occupy is the empty space I told you about. The etheric body weaves around us outwardly and grows larger and larger" (Steiner: *Die Verbindung zwischen Lebenden und Toten,* p. 44). In a lecture in Vienna on April 13, 1914, Rudolf Steiner spoke with special emphasis about the connection that exists between the experiences of "emptiness" (or the falling away of the physical body) and the etheric tableau of memory. In the course of a lengthy explanation, he said: "From the perspective of inwardness, the experience is roughly like this: Someone who has passed through the portal of death is now entirely filled with the thought, Yes, you have left your body. From now on, in the spiritual world, this body consists of pure will. It is a will-star, a star with will as its substance. This will shines with warmth: In the cosmic spaces into which you have poured yourself out, it shows you your own life between birth and death in the form of a great tableau. You owe the possibility of lingering inside this star to having drawn as much as possible from the world on the physical plane, because this will-star that now forms the background is the spiritual aspect of your physical body, the spirit that pervaded your physical body with strength. The wisdom radiating toward you is the activity or mobility of your etheric body. [...] We also have a clear inner consciousness that the presence of the will-star in the background, in this tableau of memory, is what we achieved for ourselves in

our most recent earthly life." (*Inneres Wesen des Menschen und Leben zwischen Tod und neuer Geburt*, pp. 147/148).

285 Steiner: *Die Verbindung zwischen Lebenden und Toten*, p. 23.

286 Ibid., p. 31.

287 In Dornach on September 5, 1915, Rudolf Steiner said in this context: "When our astral body enters the physical and etheric bodies each morning when we wake up, it must adapt to what these bodies have become as the result of the prior incarnation. It encounters everything we have become. When the astral body enters the etheric body, it can never make use of what the etheric body has become only in the present incarnation. It can, however, do so after death. After death the astral body is connected with the etheric body in such a way that it senses or perceives all the outcomes or results of the life that has just ended. When the astral body then separates from the etheric body after a few days, it contains the entire result of a lifetime. It extracts this result from the etheric body during the few days it spends in that body. To experience the entire result or outcome of a lifetime, the astral body does not need to spend more than a few days in the etheric body, now separated from the physical body." (*Zufall, Notwendigkeit und Vorsehung. Imaginative Erkenntnis und Vorgänge nach dem Tode*, p. 114).

288 The qualities of warmth and cold in the dissolution of the astral organization are a repeated theme in many of Rudolf Steiner's mantric verses to accompany the deceased (cf. CW 268). He describes these qualities not only in the characteristic stages of life after death in his *Theosophie* (pp. 88ff.) but also in lectures, including one given in Stuttgart on November 23, 1915, where he points out that the development of the etheric "life tableau" and its subsequent integration into the cosmos are accompanied by qualities of light and sound, whereas the process of overcoming and setting aside the astral body takes place in the sphere of warmth. In this lecture, he describes this process in detail, beginning with the dissolution of the etheric body: "First it is as

if our innermost dream of our life is enlivened, becoming a living universe, a living cosmos. Then it is filled with what we might call the 'music of the spheres.' The music of the spheres resounds throughout this dream of our life. We experience what we were between birth and death as a section of the cosmos that is now absorbed into the cosmos—not into the earthly world, where we spent the time between birth and death, but into the non-earthly world. The next thing we feel is how intimately the cosmos pervades our 'section.' We get the feeling that a light is going on within, illumining what we were. All of this flows and resounds through the panorama of our life. These processes all take place while the individual is still united with the etheric body, but then the etheric body frees itself and falls away. We experience setting aside the etheric body as leaving not only the earth and its material aspect but also its immediate surrounding, namely, light. We leave behind the earth's dense substantiality, which made the music of the spheres inaudible. Then comes a very significant final impression—which then persists—namely, the impression of having left behind the habit of allowing yourself and your surroundings to be illuminated by external light. [...] After death, once we know we are free of the etheric body, we realize that the sunlight we know from physical life exists only in the earth's field of activity. We perceive that this light is no longer distracting us. Internally generated light now fills what was first filled with sound. The inner light becomes active only because the outer light is no longer there to disrupt it. Now, when we lay aside the etheric body, we begin to enter the world that is often called kamaloka. We will call it the soul world. Enlivening from within appears first, followed by resounding from within and then by what feels like warming from within. Here on earth, we are warmed through by warmth we receive from outside; in the physical body, we feel dependent on outer warmth. Now, however, warming from within appears. In the element in which we are now living, we feel capable of calling up in ourselves a sensation we formerly received from outside. At this point, we enter a completely new element." (*Die geistigen Hintergründe des Ersten Weltkrieges*, p. 96f./102f.

289   In earthly life between birth and death, we experience enjoyment and suffering; we live in our passions and develop will impulses through the body, which serves as the vehicle for the feeling and willing soul. The forces inherent in feeling and will, however, can never really manifest completely through the body. No matter how old we become, we always feel that we could have enjoyed more, suffered more, developed more will impulses before dying. These opportunities for feeling and willing that still remain in the soul must first be overcome. Until they are overcome completely, our connection to our past earthly life is one of desire. It is as if we were looking back on this most recent earthly life. I have often described what happens next in rather trivial terms, as "breaking oneself of the habits" that connect us to physical life on earth. [...] When we fall asleep each night after the events of the day, we then spend the time between falling asleep and reawakening in our soul-spiritual aspect, outside of the body. We return because that soul-spiritual aspect feels the urge or the desire to return to the body. It is absolutely true that we experience desire for the body. Anyone who can experience the waking process consciously knows, you will wake up and you must want to wake up. Our soul-spiritual aspect is attracted to the body. This attraction must gradually fade away until it is totally overcome, in a process that takes decades. During this time, as we are gradually overcoming our connection to earthly life, we experience all of the events of that period after death in a roundabout way, through our earthly life. (*Inneres Wesen des Menschen und Leben zwischen Tod und neuer Geburt*, p. 152f.). In particular, see also Rudolf Steiner's extensive descriptions of the stages of this decade-long process in his book *Theosophie* (pp. 83ff.).

290   Steiner: (*Inneres Wesen des Menschen und Leben zwischen Tod und neuer Geburt*, p. 53f.

291   Ibid., p. 54.

292 Ibid., p. 55.

293 "To give an example, let's assume a man has passed through the portal of death and his review of life has been completed. Now that individual's connections with the previous earthly life have been sundered. Suppose someone he loves is still alive in a physical body. At the above-mentioned stage of experience, he cannot directly behold the soul that is still on earth, but a certain shift occurs: In our last life, we loved a certain person who remains behind; now we gaze on that feeling of love. Feelings are our outer world." (*Inneres Wesen des Menschen und Leben zwischen Tod und neuer Geburt*, p. 55).

294 Steiner, *Initiations-Erkenntnis*, p. 20. "Figuratively speaking, we can say that it 'goes away' after death. In reality, however, it *remains behind*. Time turns around and comes back to its starting point. We might say that the divine world actually stays where it was in the beginning while human beings periodically leave it and then return, bringing with them what they conquered for themselves outside the divine world." (*Menschenwesen, Menschenschicksal und Welt-Entwickelung*, p. 20).

295 Steiner: *Die Verbindung zwischen Lebenden und Toten*, p. 78.

296 In a certain respect, as Rudolf Steiner pointed out in many lectures, this recapitulation represents the total of nightly astral experiences during a lifetime, which recapitulated the events in the person's day from the perspective of the surroundings affected by them. In Kristiania (Helsinki) on May 16, 1923, contrasting the review process after death with the preceding experience of the etheric "thought tableau," Rudolf Steiner said: "Three days after death, our daytime experiences evaporate. Then, in a period equal to about one third of our earthly lifetime, we review our life in reverse. This is when we actually become fully conscious of our worth as a human being. What we once went through unconsciously every night emerges in full consciousness now that the etheric body has been laid aside." (*Menschenwesen, Menschenschicksal und Welt-Entwickelung*, p. 19).

297 Concerning this matter, Rudolf Steiner wrote in the spring
of 1924: "After laying aside the etheric body, the human
being is left with the astral body and the I. As long as the
astral body persists, it permits conscious experience of the
unconscious contents of the sleeping soul during earthly life.
These contents include judgments imprinted on the astral
body during sleep by spirit beings of a higher world, beings
hidden from our earthly consciousness. When we relive our
earthly experiences after death, the conscious contents of the
soul consist of judgments of our doing and thinking from
the perspective of the spirit world" (*Anthroposophische
Leitsätze*, p. 25). In September 1922, he had described the
same content as follows: "In this state, we behold ourselves
as moral figures, just as we saw ourselves as physical figures in earthly existence. Our inner aspect is now shaped
by the moral quality of our earthly activity. We behold our
moral, astral organism, which is illuminated by the spiritual,
cosmic world. Everything that world had to say about our
actions in earthly existence now stands before the human
soul as a factual image. [...] After death, we experience the
developing moral core of a future cosmos that is growing
in the womb of the cosmos. Unlike the present purely
natural order, it will have both natural and moral expres-
sions. The basic feeling passing through the soul during this
experience in a developing cosmic world is provided by the
question: In a future existence, will I be worthy of a place
in the moral and natural world order?" (*Drei Schritte der
Anthroposophie: Philosophie, Kosmologie, Religion*, p.75f;
see also *Die Philosophie, Kosmologie und Religion in der
Anthroposophie*, p. 153f.).

298 "After death, you experience the effects of whatever you
did in life, and you respond by engendering within yourself
forces that will balance out what others suffered as a consequence of your actions. In other words, through this reversal
of experience in soul territory, you absorb the power to undo
what someone suffered because of you, resulting in the desire
to be together with that person in earthly life in order to

balance out what you did. This experience in reverse engenders all the forces of compensatory karma. That is what we absorb here.

Thus the germ of karmic compensation is already engendered in the first few years or decades after we pass through the portal of death. A germinating sprout contains forces of growth that will later come to expression in the flower. Similarly, in the time after passing through the portal of death, we find the roots of a force that will persist for an entire life between death and a new birth and come to expression in the next earthly life or subsequent earthly lives as karmic compensation for what we once did. This is how the unconscious will that becomes karma is engendered" (*Die geistigen Hintergründe des Ersten Weltkrieges*, p. 195f.). See also *Anthroposophische Leitsätze*, p. 39: "In a time roughly equal to one third of the earthly life just completed, the soul experiences in spirit the necessary effects of the past earthly life from the perspective of an ethically just world order. In line with this experience, this most recent earthly life produces the intention to deliver compensation in the next earthly life, which is shaped accordingly." In addition, however, Rudolf Steiner suggests that will impulses for a compensatory reincarnation arise already from the preceding experience of the incorporation of the individualized etheric body—and with it the past incarnation's thought activity (see above) into the cosmic world ether. He spoke to this effect in Dornach on August 27, 1916: "Initially after passing through death, we entrench ourselves in our etheric body and carry it forth into the general substantiality of the world. This experience alters gradually as we go through repeated earthly lives. Just imagine everything a person thinks! Wouldn't it be the most terrible thing you could imagine if all of your thoughts were objectively embedded in the substance of the world, where they would persist for eternity? That is what would happen, however, if our repeated earthly lives did not enable us to correct thoughts that should not be allowed to persist—that is, to either correct them or to expunge them entirely, replace them with others, and so on. This is what evolution accomplishes through different earthly lives: It puts us in a position to actually improve what we imprint on the general substantiality of the world at each death. By the time we pass through our final earthly incarnation, we can strive to transmit to the substance of the world only what can really remain." (*Das Rätsel des Menschen. Die geistigen Hintergründe der menschlichen Geschichte*, p. 208).

299 "Just as the physical body is laid aside at death and the etheric body shortly thereafter, the part of the astral body that can survive only in consciousness of the outer physical world now also dissipates. Suprasensible perception, therefore, perceives three corpses: the physical, the etheric, and the astral." (*Geheimwissenschaft im Umriss*, p. 105).

300 Steiner: *Die Verbindung zwischen Lebenden und Toten*, p. 79.

301 Steiner: *Theosophie*, p. 85f./88. For textual variants of this passage, see the work cited in note 232, pp. 132/136.

302 On the supportive role of the Christ in the transition from the "soul world" to the "spirit world," cf. in particular Rudolf Steiner's explanations in his lecture in Dornach on September 14, 1922: "Durch Christi Tat wird die Menschenseele beim Übergang aus der Seelenwelt in das Geisterland gereinigt." (*Die Philosophie, Kosmologie und Religion in der Anthroposophie*, p. 156ff.).

303 Steiner: *Die Verbindung zwischen Lebenden und Toten*, p. 80.

304 In Penmaenmawr, Rudolf Steiner characterized the direct transition from the "soul world" to the "spirit world" in these words (among others): "Until the end of the reversed experience of the nights, human beings experience what they have become and what they signify for the cosmos. Now, however, they must experience what happened to the *earth itself* as a result of their lives. This process takes a very long time." (*Initiations-Erkenntnis*, p. 167; italics added).

305 On December 9, 1917, in Dornach, Rudolf Steiner spoke at length about the posthumous experience of *life* after the (necessary) destruction of the earthly element: "More than

we can say, death—the destruction of the living—is inter-woven with human actions because these actions between birth and death are so completely enmeshed in sensory existence." After death, the dead develop "life-awareness," and the human soul adapts completely to "preserving the holiness of life, to pervading the living with more and more life." (*Geschichtliche Notwendigkeit und Freiheit. Schicksalseinwirkungen aus der Welt der Toten*, p. 45ff.).

Literature Cited

Works by Rudolf Steiner referred to in the text and notes, listed in English when available. All German titles are from the Rudolf Steiner Gesamtausgabe, published by Rudolf Steiner Verlag, Dornach, Switzerland.

GA 9   *Theosophy.* Tr. Catherine E. Creeger. Great Barrington, MA: SteinerBooks 1994. In German: *Theosophie.*

GA 13   *An Outline of Esoteric Science.* Tr. Catherine E. Creeger. Great Barrington, MA: SteinerBooks 1997. In German: *Die Geheimwissenschaft im Umriss.*

GA 25   *Drei Schritte der Anthroposophie. Philosophie–Kosmologie–Religion* [Three steps of anthroposophy. Philosophy–cosmology–religion] (1922). 4. Auflage 1999. (See also GA 215, in English: *Philosophy, Cosmology and Religion.* Tr. Lisa Monges and D. Bugbey. Spring Valley, NY: Anthroposophic Press 1984).

GA 26   *Anthroposophical Leading Thoughts.* Tr. George and Mary Adams. Forest Row, England: Rudolf Steiner Press 1998. In German: *Anthroposophische Leitsätze.*

GA 28   *Autobiography: Chapters in the Course of My Life. (1861-1907)* Tr. Rita Stebbing. Notes and chronology Paul M. Allen. Great Barrington, MA: SteinerBooks 2006. In German: *Mein Lebensgang.*

GA 95   *Founding a Science of the Spirit.* Tr. revised M. Barton. Forest Row, England: Rudolf Steiner Press 1999. In German: *Vor dem Tore der Theosophie.*

GA 99   *Rosicrucian Wisdom.* Tr. revised J. Collis. Forest Row, England: Rudolf Steiner Press 2000. (Previously published as *Theosophy of the Rosicrucian*). In German: *Die Theosophie des Rosenkreuzers.*

GA 131 *From Jesus to Christ.* Tr. Charles Davy. Forest Row, England: Rudolf Steiner Press 2005. In German: *Von Jesus zu Christus.*

GA 140   *Life between Death and Rebirth.* Tr. René Querido. Great
Barrington, MA: SteinerBooks/Anthroposophic Press 1968.
In German: *Okkulte Untersuchungen über das Leben
zwischen Tod und neuer Geburt.*

GA 141   *Das Leben zwischen dem Tode und der neuen Geburt im
Verhältnis zu den kosmischen Tatsachen* [Life between
death and new birth in relationship to cosmic facts]
(1912/13). 5. Auflage 1997.

GA 148   *The Fifth Gospel. From the Akashic Record.* Tr. A. R.
Meuss. Forest Row, England: Rudolf Steiner Press 2007.
In German: *Aus der Akasha-Chronik.*

GA 150   *Die Welt des Geistes und ihr Hereinragen in das physische Dasein* [The World of the spirit and its extension
into the physical world.]. 2. Auflage 1980.

GA 153   *The Inner Nature of Man and Our Life between Death
and Rebirth.* Tr. Anna Meuss. Forest Row, England:
Rudolf Steiner Press 1994. In German: *Inneres Wesen des
Menschen und Leben zwischen Tod und neuer Geburt.*

GA 154   *The Presence of the Dead on the Spiritual Path.* Tr.
Christian von Arnim. Hudson, NY: Anthroposophic
Press 1990. In German: *Wie erwirbt man sich Verständnis
fur die geistige Welt?*

GA 157   *The Destinies of Individuals and of Nations.* Tr. Anna
R. Meuss. Spring Valley, New York: Anthroposophic
Press 1986. In German: *Menschenschicksale und
Völkerschichsale.*

GA 157a   *Schicksalsbildung und Leben nach Tode* [The Formation of
destiny and the life after death] (1915). 3. Auflage 1981.

GA 159   *Das Geheimnis des Todes.* [The mystery of death] (1915).
2. Auflage 1980.

GA 161   *Wege der geistigen Erkenntnis und der Erneuerung
der künstlerischen Weltenschauung* [Paths of spiritual
knowledge and the renewal of the artistic worldview]
(1915). 2. Auflage 1999.

GA 163   *Chance, Providence, and Necessity.* Tr. Marjorie Spock.
Hudson, NY: Anthroposophic Press 1988. In German:
*Zufall, Notwendigkeit und Vorsehung. Imaginative
Erkenntnis und Vorgänge nach dem Tode.*

GA 168   *Die Verbindung zwischen Lebenden und Toten* [The connection between the living and the dead] (1916). 4. Auflage 1995.

GA 170   *The Riddle of Humanity.* Tr. John F. Logan. London: Rudolf Steiner Press 1990. In German: *Rätsel des Menschen. Die geistigen Hintergründe der menschlichen Geschichte.*

GA 174a   *Mitteleuropa zwischen Ost und West* [Middle Europe between east and west]. (1914-18). 2. Auflage 1982.

GA 174b   *Die geistigen Hintergründe des Ersten Weltkrieges* (1914-18/1921) [The spiritual background of the First World War]. 2. Auflage 1994.

GA 176   *Aspects of Human Evolution.* Tr. Rita Stebbing. Hudson, NY: Anthroposophic Press 1987. In German: *Menschliche und menschheitliche Entwicklungswahrheiten.*

GA 178   *Secret Brotherhoods and the Mystery of the Human Double.* Tr. J. Collis. Forest Row, England: Rudolf Steiner Press 2004. In German: *Individuelle Geistwesen und ihr wirken in der seele des Menschen.*

GA 179   *The Influence of the Dead on Destiny.* Tr. revised Marsha Post. Great Barrington, MA: SteinerBooks 2007. In German: *Geschichtliche Notwendigkeit und Freiheit.*

GA 182   *Death as Metamorphosis of Life.* Tr. Sabine Seiler. Great Barrington, MA: SteinerBooks 2008. In German: *Der Tod als lebenswandlung.*

GA 191   *Soziales Verstandnis aus geisteswissenschaftlicher Erkenntnis* [Social understanding from spiritual scientific cognition] (1919). 3. Auflage 1989. (See also *The Influences of Lucifer and Ahriman.* Tr. D. S. Osmond. Hudson, NY: Anthroposophic Press 1993).

GA 193   *The Esoteric Aspect of the Social Question.* Tr. P. Wehrle. Forest Row, England: Rudolf Steiner Press 2001. In German: *Der innere Aspekt des Sozialen Rätsels.*

GA 206   *Man as a Being of Sense and Perception.* Tr. Dorothy Lenn. Vancouver, Canada: Steiner Book Centre 1981. In German: *Menschenwerden, Weltenseele und Weltengeist. 2 Teil.*

GA 209   *Nordische und mitteleuropäische Geistimpulse* [Nordic and Central European spiritual impulses] (1921). 2. Auflage 1982.

GA 215   *Philosophy, Cosmology and Religion.* Tr. L. Monges
          and D. Bugbey. Revised M. St. Goar. Edit. Stewart
          Easton. Spring Valley, NY: Anthroposophic Press 1984.
          In German: *Die Philosophie, Kosmologie und Religion in
          der Anthroposophie.*

GA 218   *Geistige Zusammenhänge in der Gestaltung des mensch-
          lichen Organismus* (1922) [Spiritual connections in the
          forming of the human organism]. 3. Auflage 1992.

GA 224   *Die menschliche Seele in ihrem Zusammenhang mit gött-
          lich-geistigen Individualitaten.* [The human soul and its
          connection with divine-spiritual individualities] (1923).
          3. Auflage 1992.

GA 226   *Man's Being, His Destiny, and World-Evolution.* Tr. Erna
          McArthur. Spring Valley, NY: Anthroposophic Press 1984.
          In German: *Menschenwesen, Menschenschicksal und Welt-
          Entwicklung.*

GA 227   *The Evolution of Consciousness as Revealed through
          Initiation Knowledge.* Tr. V. E. Watkin and C. Davy.
          Forest Row, England: Rudolf Steiner Press 2007. In
          German: *Initiations-Erkenntnis.*

GA 231   *At Home in the Universe.* Tr. H. Collison. Hudson,
          NY: Anthroposophic Press 2000. (Previously published
          as *Supersensible Man*). In German: *Der übersinnliche
          Mensch, anthroposophisch erfasst.*

GA 236   *Karmic Relationships Vol 2.* Tr. George Adams.
          Revised M. Cotterell, C. Davy, D. S. Osmond. London:
          Rudolf Steiner Press 1997.   In German: *Esoterische
          Betrachtungen karmischer Zusammenhänge II.*

GA 260a   *The Constitution of the School of Spiritual Science.* Tr.
          G. Adams and J. & S. Rudel. London: Rudolf Steiner
          Press 1980. See also *The Foundation Stone/The Life,
          Nature and Cultivation of Anthroposophy.* London:
          Rudolf Steiner Press 1996). In German: *Die Konstitution
          der Allgemeinen Anthroposophischen Gellschaft und der
          Freien Hochschule fur Geisteswissenschaft.*

GA 261   *Unsere Toten* [Our dead. Addresses, words of remembrances,
          and meditative verses] (1906-1924). 2. Auflage 1964.

GA 264   *From the History and Contents of the First Section of the Esoteric School 1904-1914.* Tr. John Wood. Great Barrington, MA: SteinerBooks 2010.

GA 268   *Mantrische Sprüche. Seelenübungen II* (Soul exercises. Vol. 2) (1903-1925). 1. Auflage 1999.

GA 270b   *Esoterische Unterweisungen für die erste Klasse der Freien Hochschule für Geisteswissenschafte am Goetheanum 1924.* [Esoteric instructions for the first class of the School for Spiritual Science at the Goetheanum]. II Band. 2. Auflage 1999.

GA 287   *Der Dornacher Bau als Wahrzeichen geschichtlichen Werdens und künstlerischer umwandlungsimpulse* [The Building in Dornach as a symbol of historical becoming] (1914). 2. Auflage 1985.

GA 293   *The Foundations of Human Experience* Tr. Robert Lathe and Nancy Whittaker. Great Barrington, MA: SteinerBooks 1996. In German: *Allgemeine Menschenkunde als Grundlage der Pädagogik.*

GA 316   *Course for Young Doctors.* Spring Valley, NY: Mercury Press 1997. In German: *Meditative Betrachtungen und Anleitungen zur Vertiefung der Heilkunst.*

GA 319   *The Healing Process. Spirit, Nature & Our Bodies.* Tr. Catherine Creeger. Great Barrington, MA: SteinerBooks 2010. In German: *Anthroposophische Menschenerkenntnis und Medizin.*

GA 334   *Social Issues. Meditative Thinking & the Threefold Social Order.* Tr. Joe Reuter. Revised by Sabine H. Seiler. Hudson, NY: Anthroposophic Press 1991. In German: *Vom Einheitsstaat zum dreigliedrigen sozialen Organismus.*

GA 343   *Spirituelles Erkennen. Religioses Empfinden. Kultisches Handeln. Vorträge und Kurse über christlich-religiöses Wirken II* [Spiritual knowledge. Religious feeling. Ritual doing. Lectures and courses on Christian religious work. Vol. 2] (1921). 1. Auflage 1993.

GA 345   *Vom Wesen des wirken Wortes. Vorträge und Kurse über christlich-religiöses Wirken IV* [Concerning the nature of the working word. Lectures and courses on Christian religious work. Vol. 4] (1923). 1. Auflage 1994.

Sources of the Illustrations

Ita Wegman Institute
for Basic Research into Anthroposophy

PFEFFINGER WEG 1 A CH-4144 ARLESHEIM, SWITZERLAND

www.wegmaninstitut.ch

e-mail: sekretariat@wegmaninstitut.ch

The Ita Wegman Institute for Basic Research into Anthroposophy is a non-profit research and teaching organization. It undertakes basic research into the lifework of Dr. Rudolf Steiner (1861–1925) and the application of Anthroposophy in specific areas of life, especially medicine, education, and curative education. Work carried out by the Institute is supported by a number of foundations and organizations and an international group of friends and supporters. The Director of the Institute is Prof. Dr. Peter Selg.